Hear Through the Silence

By Jennifer Wenn

CONTENTS

Beginnings

Lost Songs

*Maybe the desire to make something beautiful
is the piece of God that is inside each of us*
Mary Oliver, "Franz Marc's Blue Horses"

Once I wrote songs,
was young and didn't know any better,
aspired to an unreachable fantasy,
to a person I couldn't then be.
Immature fragile tunes
and gossamer words
soon lost in a cacophony
of mocking laughter from
without and within,
drowned out by blasts of
seriousness reasonableness conformity,
naïve notes distorted into an
unending metronomic drumbeat of
analytics and logic and practicality;
the songs shattered, scattered on the winds
of uncounted delicate melodies
never given voice, throats and souls
strangled by fear and acquiescence.

Is that the end? Divine spark forever
sublimated or smothered? Sometimes.
But maybe, a lifetime later,
the quixotic urge returns unbidden,
the primordial quest for beauty reborn,
habit and convention cast aside
and the fragments of long-ago dreams
reforged with hard-won tools,
perhaps, one autumn day, to sound a
hopeful transfigured echo of long-lost songs.

Whitman/Monet

May I call you Walt and Claude?
That's very familiar, I realize,
but I feel I know you, intimately after a fashion.
The Poet, with your vocabulary, your lists,
exulting the everyday, but seeing
much more through and beyond,
joyfully singing the body electric,
claiming all humankind as brothers and sisters,
dancing through time,
immersing in your Leaves becomes wonderful meditation.
The Painter, playing with light,
subjects as deceptively simple as a wheatstack,
or as vaulting as a cathedral,
shades of meaning within the changing sun and fog,
finding magic and insight in water lilies,
claiming everything around you as worthy of adoration,
falling into your Impressions a mystical experience.
One, a painter with language,
the other, a poet with brush and canvas,
two great spirits entwined by
profound vision and seductive simplicity.
I claim you as muses, as ideals,
not to be achieved, but, perhaps,
approached, in my own way.

Words

I
Mysterious, mystical, and yet material:
Words, language, source of untold power,
Power to bridge, power to divide,
Power to bind, power to sever,
Power to heal, power to wound;
Magnificent gift, awesome responsibility.

II
Forcing their way to the surface
From depths unknown,
Modulated by my spirit,
Hesitatingly, delayed,
And yet inevitable,
Finally moulding into my own unique voice.

Discoveries

Contentedly plopped on the front lawn,
my toddler soul registering warmth
and the security of home,
venturing today nearly to the curb,
feeling the smooth-sided, gently
rough-edged grass, and needing
the texture in my mouth,
enjoying the taste, happily immersed
in my new discovery.
Then startled by a taller, familiar figure
dashing out the front door,
hollering stop, emanating waves of disgust,
expostulating all manner of
dire potential consequence,
throwing up a barrier between me
and the world around,
exploration time at an end;
the grass will never seem the same.

Strawberry Picking

Rumbling by the strip mall
and apartment buildings,
cursing traffic lights
and idiot drivers, a
peripheral phantom beckons,
the strawberry patch,
a young parent passing on
traditions, slowing childhood
impatience to simple pleasures in
soil, leaf and fruit.
The farmer resignedly talks
about the pressure to sell,
"development" steamrolling in.
Half listening, I glance down
the row and sense the
sun-dappled inchoate me,
plunked in my chosen spot.
While most gad about
and fill baskets,
I search and shift slowly,
carefully studying each candidate.
Imperfections—they remain here;
too much colour—their time has passed;
too little—their moment is yet to come.
Bit by bit building a little mound of
succulent scarlet perfection,
eschewing others' lack of standards,
struggling on with a vision
of epicurean ecstasy and
a quest for rare beauty,
just a sigh of distant thunder
floating on the breeze.

Singing in my Heart

Houses and streets and parks
gaily festooned with seasonal cheer;
concert hall, skilled carollers
serenade with holiday chestnuts
secular and sacred.
Sing-along time arrives,
voices of one and all rise in
joyful chorus; I remain mute,
throat closed by an old memory,
but in my heart I'm singing.

In a flash, transported back
through the decades by my own
Ghost of Christmas Past,
I hover over my eleven-year old self,
and see, I loved to sing, happily
one of the school choir,
practicing all fall, excited as
holiday concert crept ever closer.
Day arrives, choir master sidles up,
asks if I wouldn't rather
turn music sheets for the soloist.
Young I was, but not stupid,
saw right through the thin veneer
to the plain meaning:
My voice was not wanted.
But *No* I said, thinking,
I've practiced all fall, and on I sang...
for that one day; thereafter
voice cut off or reduced to a murmur
I hoped no one else could hear,
I shared it in public no more;
but in my heart I was singing.

In a breath, in the twinkling of an eye
I am back, voices young and old
still happily joined together,
and I – I listen;
but I am singing in my heart,
loud and clear and sublime.

Sistine Chapel

A lifetime ago, and yet yesterday,
Rome, the Eternal City, another station
on the family European pilgrimage.
A fierce sun gazing on as we wandered
through remains of long ago lives,
shadows of ancient grandeur,
my teens about to dawn, but still
fascinated by the stony memories.

Our path leading to St. Peter's,
soaring heavenward,
symbol of immense mastery and
wealth cloaking devotion,
centuries of worship echoing
amongst the artistic ecstasies,
awesome lodestar of a faith not mine.

Inevitably to the Sistine Chapel;
Michelangelo's eternal ambition
blazing duskily forth.
Overpowered by a seismic shift,
swept off my feet by an
indefinable tsunami and sitting,
gazing upward in dazed contemplation,
lacking context but intuitively knowing,
groping for words through a feeling designated as
I've been here before.
Not a picture, not television, not a movie.
Here.

And still, even now, I turn it over
in my heart, sensing across the decades
an overwhelming presence,

me the callow, improbable medium;
looking back along my unmeasured
search for meaning, and knowing
Lao Tzu's truth: it began with a single step,
the one across that threshold from
the domain of ecclesiastical and temporal power
into the realm of ravishing divine genius.

Intrusion

Transgender Anthem

Since time immemorial,
revealed or hidden,
self-aware or suppressed,
we have been here.

Through pain, confusion and joy,
tearing at contrary, shrouding shells,
we have been here.

We follow paths
indescribable and incredible,
yearning to shine forth
our extraordinary iridescence,
and we are here.

We are the convention-shakers,
       mould-breakers,
       trailblazers,
and we are here!

We are not an illness
       or a theory
       or a debating point;
We are flesh and blood,
marvellous souls and children of the cosmos,
and we are here!

We are dismissed by the ignorant,
       stared at by the fear-blind,
       assailed because we dare to
       disturb comfortable prejudices,
but we are here!

We are scared yet courageous,
    despised yet loved,
    weary yet striding on,
and we are here!

We are children and parents,
    siblings and spouses,
    friends and lovers,
    colleagues and neighbours,
    poor and well-off,
and we are here!

Hatred fells some of us
but we remain unshakeable
        unbreakable
    bright, blazing beacons of
    a new, rediscovered spirit,
and we absolutely,
    emphatically,
    now and forever
Will Be Here!

Anne

The mists enveloping childhood part a bit,
and I see us, aged seven,
simply, fondly, chatting
in the abandoned schoolyard,
you, a girl; me a boy,
or, at least, so it seemed;
so everyone told me, and so
the bodily container signified.
Convention said we shouldn't be friends,
not at that age; but we were,
and something more.
A magical resonance, not understood,
at least by me, until long afterward.
From a half century's perspective
I see the incipient self, perceiving in you,
without awareness then,
myself—the part trapped within
the shell and expectation.
And you? You were kind, gently
handling the butterfly you somehow
sensed within the cocoon.

I moved, we parted, until
a decade and half later,
a chance meeting on a bus:
You, a beautiful grown woman;
me, a more mature masculine exterior
unconscious of the feminine within.
Brief words, the link still there, final(?) parting.

The woman now finally emerging here,
finding her voice,
hopes the years have been kind

and across time and whatever distance,
appreciating only now your pure,
extraordinary gift of that faraway time,
would like to lift your soul a little bit,
and say, simply, *thank you.Anne.*

Tic

They moved in
one at a time at first,
each not a tick with a k,
the solid Middle English word,
with companion tock
metronomic, predictable;
rather, T-I-C, exotic,
French and Italian roots,
spasmodic, explosive.
Not, doctors to the contrary, a habit;
not, contravening others, a ploy for attention;
not a spasm or a twitch,
a deeper urge, head, eyes, neck and more
jumping and jerking about, control
given over to a mad marionetteer
intent on a mobile sideshow
to lure mockery and insult,
induce isolation and pain
physical and emotional.
Stress-magnified, neurological
wiring crossed they say now,
but look within my boy-husk
and see in each spastic jolt a
a silent scream from
a girlhood denied,
a lament for a child
pushed to the margin.

Slowly gentled, some,
by passing decades,
and more by the girl's eventual
ascension into light,
but havoc bequeathed on

overstrained neck,
and an outsider's view induced,
now by dilatory grace transmuted
to a poet's attempted lines,
wielding and assuaging the past,
but never, ever forgetting.

David

It was different back then, mid '70s, high school.
Being labelled a gay male (*fag, faggot, homo*)
was a Mark of Cain interpreted by the mob
as permission to cast out from school society
(such as it was),
to bully, to torment as they saw fit.
David, you were labelled early.
Target of derision behind your back,
verbally assaulted to your face.
Thrown into the girls washroom.
Locked in a locker.
But you fought back, in your own way.
Played the fool, told rude jokes,
made yourself a gadfly.
And I? Geeky, intellectual, Tourette-twitching,
I was far outside the mainstream,
my then-male appurtenances enclosing
a sleeping identity deemed
more dangerous even than yours.
But desperate to avoid the Mark
I said, not much; and did,
nothing.

Long afterwards, my hibernating core finally
awakening, seeking light and integration,
searching memories, I wondered,
What happened to you?
Maybe a tea, or a phone call,
or at least an online connection,
reminisce, say I'm sorry.
Turning sleuth, I found your path
led to Calgary, where it seems
you found community, and joy too, I hope.

I also discovered the sad truth:
You'd passed on early one November morning,
aged just 33, following, the obituary said,
a courageous battle with HIV—
yet one more victim of that then-dread plague,
your loss mourned by your many friends.
So no apology, at least, not a conventional one.

One memory I hold onto.
By Grade 13, the final year,
you'd become something of an established fact.
Some bullies had graduated; others, perhaps, had
become bored, moved onto other targets.
The senior prom coming, both of us dateless.
Strict custom dictated that one couldn't go alone,
so, locating a modicum of courage,
mixed with some the-hell-with-them,
I approached you, and we went,
stag, as it was called, as friends.
Immodestly, I take a little solace,
a little pride, in that.

And now, I could say Rest in Peace,
but maybe something else is more appropriate.
So, wherever you are now, stand up,
be proud, know you are missed,
and mourned, by at least one from those
difficult days of youth, and, as they say,
let your freak flag nobly fly, my friend.

Mirror

I peer into the glass,
looking for the woman
I know is there, but mostly I see a
too-male shell staring back,
facial stubble never quite gone,
jaw line too strong, hair too thin,
decades of conditioning
clouding the view.
Others, some, say they see her,
but I have trouble,
the moult never to be completed.
Oh, but those magical moments
when the look is right, my soul open,
and for an instant, she's there,
for an instant I'm whole.

On Seeing the Little Shepherdess

Swimming the glorious, noisy tides of
World Pride 2014, exultant in the
blooming of my long dormant femininity,
borne along by an electric current,
immersed in a supportive sea of
companion emergent chrysalids.

Perspective soon needed, floating off
to bathe in art's calming waters and
breathe in the quiet of Toronto's AGO;
approaching Paul Peel's little nook,
like me a London, Ontario local,
best work done in exotic Paris,
taken so young, not yet thirty-two;
       my ruminations interrupted,
       flashing back twenty-seven years,
       a special exhibit in our home town,
       one painting that unfathomably wound
       a tentacle around my heart.

And there, high up on a wall,
the screen of trees in the distance,
meadow sloping down and left
to a pond just in front,
lily pads and blue irises, attendant
blossoms to the little shepherdess
bursting from the background,
seated on a large rock,
her charges grazing amongst the trees,
crook, clothes and cares cast aside,
hair garlanded with delicate pink flowers,
skin glowing with expectation,
a demurely sensual and unveiled adolescent,

quietly bold, gazing at nature's mirror
echoing her incipient beauty,
left foot curled shyly under,
right testing the pool awaiting her.

Awash in a wave of meaning, transfixed,
sinking down to contemplate this image done in oils
a century ago, but seeing my reflection.
Separated by decades in age from
the model posing outside for the first time,
this moment by more than one hundred years
from the young artist's loving strokes,
his vision's eternal youth from
my all-too-real aging flesh and blood;
but we three, model, vision and I,
still compeers, sister adventurers
setting out into vast beckoning waters.

Stares

They come in different types.
The quicker, intense flash.
The leisurely look-over,
averting your gaze if I make eye contact.
The long, lingering examination,
as of a lab specimen for your perusal,
no looking away.
Sometimes I read simply confusion,
or surprise, in your eyes.
Sometimes, a smug recognition (well, good for you).
Sometimes, though, the disgust, the contempt, is palpable.
Sometimes, I don't notice.
Sometimes, I don't care.
Sometimes, I stare back.
Other times, it hurts, once more
failing to transform the external
into a portrait of the internal,
once more exceptionalized,
not allowed to simply be.

He

He.
A little word, two letters, one short syllable;
but context is all, context confers power.
He.
Women's sauna, pre-class warm-up. A long road here,
transforming masculine name, accoutrements, habits, hair, body
(anxiety, bureaucracy, money, hormones, surgery, pain, joy),
feminine blooming the hope, the thought-to-be-achieved goal.
He.
Oh, I'd heard it before as flowering progressed,
hurt each time, and yet was healed;
but context is all, context confers power.
He.
My mostly unclothed body alongside others,
acceptance, friendly chat.
And there it was—He—in spite of all,
in spite of location and name,
in spite of exposure actual and metaphorical,
He,
not malicious, and therefore
all the more honest and wounding,
He,
trifling sound become jagged blade
plunged in to the quick and twisted,
without any intent, but, oh, with effect,
HE self-esteem self-image ripped and riven asunder,
HE illusions delusions shattered in a trice,
He.

Shock soon wearing off, too numb for tears,
humiliation creeping in like gangrene,
I slink homeward early, looking for
some dark hole to crawl into, vainly seeking comfort

as other words crowd in: misfit, freak, sideshow.
Why?

And finding that wounds may, perhaps, cover over,
but some scars run deep.

Intrusion

Black and white image coloured with meaning,
Paris, La Ville Lumière, The City of Light,
re-emerging after the ghastly darkness of World War II.
Long shadows denote a cooling summer's evening
at an outdoor café under the trees,
Champigneulles from Lorraine,
the Queen of Beers, the house beverage,
drinks and cigarettes on the tables,
music lost except to clasping dancers frozen mid-shuffle.
These men oblivious or perhaps peacock-proud,
but burning still, eyes, women's eyes:
On the left, sporting a gaily floral dress, dark sweater and
a face replete with irritation and an air of disgust,
boring into the interloper the silent, screaming questions:
WHO are YOU? WHAT are you?
A formal skirt suit centre foreground, stiff and self-conscious,
determined not to look but peripheral vision in full play.
And on the right, back a few steps, over her partner's shoulder,
piercing fear; of being exposed? of the outsider?

I've seen those looks, and others, many times
(side eye, up and down scan, double take, full on stare,
quietly pointed out, conspicuously whispered about, shouted at),
many reasons reducing to one:
I am intruding on their world, on their psyches,
an unexpected, unwanted, disturbing element.

Attempting release from the hypnotic gazes
I try to turn the page.

Dream Memorials

Ephemeral and ethereal,
        yet eloquent and laden,
one masculine figure
        materializing in the mist,
achingly and all-too familiar
        precursor reflection from
        bygone years and decades,
faded from view by the formidable,
        magnificent metamorphosis,
silently waving back while offstage voices
        reflect on a seemingly
        recent premature passing,
remembering perhaps
        sincere striving, quirks,
        accomplished yet
        haunted by a ghost of
        unfinished potential,
        times celebrated and mourned;
a vision along an abandoned heading.

Look again, and see a life-saving
relinquishment to femininity,
unforgotten male vanguard
withdrawing to a still, quiet place,
bidding success, validating the course;
our mutual benedictions:
well done good and faithful vessel,
I am with you always.

Waking, we sail on.

For A Fellow Traveller

The road is long and arduous
for some of us, inner flame
imprisoned in a contrary shell,
peeking through only far into the journey.
The miles travelled take their toll,
the body seems to betray us anew,
in other ways, breaking down, bringing pain.
I too know the dichotomy of
simultaneous revelation and disintegration;
ask questions with no answer
that can be found now;
feel in my own way I don't fit in and never will.

But I also know what it is to be inspired,
to see others like you strive on,
fight to let the fire blaze forth;
to realize that we are all
irreplaceable companions
for so many fellow travellers;
to exult in another's beautiful,
innate incandescence.

So shine on, your path lies ahead still,
and wherever it leads I'll be quietly alongside.

Victoria Peak, Hong Kong

Demons of doubt and ill-health defeated,
an arduous, amazing expedition now climaxing,
defiantly clanking up the mountainside
on the historic tram like a chariot-borne conqueror
riding to their triumph, I emerge at the top,
and the sun explodes overhead while
the fabled city spreads out below,
reaching up the heights and
yearning to embrace the vast Pacific.

Proudly beguiled and in
contemplative surprise, here I am,
a past middle-aged western tourist,
with my son, far from home,
and there, seven million strong, is the
Queen of the Pearl River delta,
the buzz and energy drifting up here
like soaring sparks from a
crackling late-summer bonfire.

Far too from my origins, now painfully,
miraculously transmuted
to the feminine, poetic and mystical,
in awed communion with
Hong Kong, once seven thousand
fisherman and charcoal burners,
claimed mid-nineteenth century by British overlords,
built into a dynamo by ambitious occidental power
and the extraordinary energy of the orient,
a triumphant fusion of East and West,
precariously balancing wealth and poverty,
seething urbanization and craggy wilderness,
now part of an immense, smothering oligarchy

but steadfastly proclaiming its unique identity
as in my turn I proclaim
here I stand, this peak have I climbed.

My Stuffed Animal

His name was Laddy,
but my toddler tongue
couldn't wrap around the L.
A foot and half long, slim,
collie, a green corduroy coat
cradling hug-worn skin,
like me designated a boy,
my constant companion
(one tragic evening left in the sandbox,
a thorough de-anting needed),
guardian against night terrors
and daytime distress,
until, thinking myself
somehow more grown up,
I set him aside to fade from my life.

Now, distaff finally released, my body having
aged and evolved and been remade,
spirit expanded, but new fears to face and
inside still a conduit to old emotions,
inside still a little girl who has
always been there and always will,
who deserves after all this time
her own special friend,
her own nocturnal companion.
So now there's Addy Junior,
a plumper textile canine, rippled in different places,
but channelling her ancestor's spirit.
And yes, my new Addy is definitely a girl too.

Triptychs

Three Haiku for Algonquin Park

1
Woodland trail beside
A stream burbling in my ear
A black fly seeks food

2
Plash of the paddle
Gently stroking round the bend
A grazing moose stares

3
Unearthly loon calls
Echo across the water
A crackling campfire

Three Haiku for Turkey Point

1
Far out, sudden gale,
Grampy's experienced hands
Guide us safely home

2
Cooking marshmallows
Watching moonrise on the bay
Embers perfect now

3
Old sandhill was here
Swallowed now by green living
Still in memory

Three Haiku for the Wisdom Path, Lantau Island, Hong Kong

1
A peaceful trail from
Bustle to entrance flitting
Butterflies beckon

2
Inscribed stelae guide
On infinity-shaped path
Ancient mountains watch

3
Script unreadable
To me Heart Sutra meaning
Flowing from all round

Three Haiku for the Galapagos

1
Ignoring me a
Hopeful blue-footed booby
Scans the horizon

2
Sally Lightfoot crab
Scuttles nimbly in vain search
Of a missing limb

3
Through volcanic scrub
Ancient tortoise languidly
Lumbers stretching time

Three Haiku for The Bruce

1
Flowerpot pillars
Stand guard, rocky balance acts
Through eons of storms

2
Escarpment-hugging
Bruce Trail forever grasping
For Manitoulin

3
Glass-bottomed tour boat's
Puttering circles disturb
Harbour shipwreck's sleep

Three Haiku for Peyto Lake

1
Sea of soaring peaks
Tourist passage hears nearby
Whispering magic

2
Rock flour patiently
Glacier-ground is employed by
The divine palette

3
Rockies hike over
Ridge, curving round, and down there—
Outlandish turquoise

Three Haiku for Visegrad, Hungary

1
Danube's endless flow
Medieval crag-mounted
Castle pays homage

2
Tourists still en route
Morning stillness calling out
Hear through the silence

3
Stone obduracy
Yields, time's illusion dissolves
Past caresses now

Storm

Ruminations

Knowing I repulse the mob,
dishonoured by mere contact,
I plunge headfirst into isolation
and jeopardize fragile spirit
with lonely ruminations.

Panic

A twinge, a small thing, something feared,
or something not understood,
noticed, leading to a thought, coupled to emotion,
growing, metastasizing, eating away all consideration,
taking over head and heart,
body responding, magnifying and multiplying:
Light headed, flushed, chest tight,
sounds and light and people too much, unreal.
Reassurance perhaps sought, told once again
"It's nothing", or, "You're fine";
or simply escaping, closing off, shutting out,
shutting down, resting fevered mind and soul.
The storm slowly recedes, leaving in its wake questions:
What happened? Why? Why again? Why now?
Will it happen yet once more?

Storm

Whether earthly or psychic
there's a rhythm to a storm.
Sensitive souls feel it first in their bones,
then, a slight shift in the breeze,
rising wind on a fine day.
Darkening clouds begin to gather,
far-off rumble, flashes in the distance.
First drops, shelter sought on the run.
A blinding bolt, a breath later
the first ferocious crack splitting the air,
bringing sheets of rain, streets turned to streams,
howling gale whipping mighty oaks,
one and all helpless before the
gathering, endless-seeming power and fury.

Then, not noticed till passed,
an inflection point,
a fragile diminution of the deluge,
a subtle brightening suffusing the air.
Flash and clap separate and fade,
recovery gathers force,
kinder drafts move in,
sun reasserts herself,
birdsong heralds storm's end.
In its wake broken branches,
or perhaps worse, or perhaps simply
a memory at once unforgettable and unreal.

Dawn

Hale afternoons modulate
cheerless mornings,
fading to a longing to tarry over
the clemency of quiescent evenings,
but on we drive to nightmares
which infest sleep, hoping to score
a peaceful, floating variant
to carry us to dawn.

Demons

Defences down, they slip in at night,
ready for morning,
thieving in tandem peace of mind:
Regret for what was not, or was;
fear of what might be, or might not be;
together crowding out the now,
two demons to be daily pushed away,
who then duly plot their return.
Daily too the nurturing of now;
timid soul, may she flourish and grow,
one day to perform the exorcism.

Down the Rabbit Hole

With thanks to Lewis Carroll

Alice's rabbit hole was across a field
and under the hedge, where she found
a Wonderland of strange beings—
chronometrically-obsessed rabbits,
off-kilter tea parties, smirking cats,
obstreperous playing cards.
Unseen is mine, but very real.
Sometimes I trip over an ethereal rock
and stumble in unwillingly;
at others, intrepid spelunker, I seek the way.

Different turnings lie in wait.
Down one, shards of startling light,
seductive voices from the cold rocks
hiss forebodings familiar, and strange,
new, and echoes from long ago,
urging me to quake and cower.
In another, a cloying and oppressive
miasma ingesting illumination,
dark vaporous entangling tendrils
coaxing me to sink down inert and remain.

There is yet another passage, clothed at once
in spring greens and autumn golds,
quiet except for soft birdsong,
or perhaps the gentle crackle of a warming fire.
For a precious interval dissonance abates, mists clear,
all is peacefully revealed, while time stands still.

Night Flights

With thanks to Emily Dickinson

As the sun's slipping past the horizon
bestows slumber on day's brightness
unveiling night's shadows and myriad scintillations,
so when consciousness fades,
reason rests, liberating deeper and subtler currents.
By intuition, Emily writes,
Mightiest Things assert themselves,
and potent indeed are night's perils and possibilities
when the soul takes flight on
wings unshackled from logicality.

Base instinct, innate or long-ago induced,
primitive and fear-based, sweeps and dives
through dreamscapes harrowing and confusing,
a dread funhouse ride cacophonous,
labyrinthine and exhausting.

Another course, Emily's true intuition,
a calm, connected knowing
like an infant gazing into their parent's eyes,
is easily swept away, but when flown proves
quietly miraculous, a peaceful reaching out,
soaring on starfire through infinities,
a treasured gift of stillness.

Wakefulness resuming, night flights
left behind but the unconscious
mementos remain, some needing release,
others to be embraced.
Potent indeed are night's perils and possibilities
when the soul takes flight on unshackled wings.

Hatchlings

Fetal, cowering under a black haze,
shrinking from the oncoming day
insistently knocking at the window,
when comes the lure of the familiar burble:
My daughter, reaching out from half
a world away, texting evening pictures
from a Sri Lankan beach, tiny baby turtles
pushing up through the sand, breaking free,
past the hand-lettered sign carefully marking
place and Christmas Eve embedding.
Another burble, more images from her,
little ones skittering to the ocean
to claim their place. Entranced,
she celebrates her joy and wonder,
transporting me, and I am there too, witnessing
new hope taking its first steps.

Bravery

Bravest acts are not
necessarily witnessed
or given medals
but
transpire unseen as
the scattered fearful army
of overwrought souls
rises
once more to battle
with another day.

Once Upon a Weekday Morning

For Edgar Allen Poe

It is not a good start to the day.
But then, I am not now, nor have
ever been, a morning person.
Fears, anxieties, dimly-remembered
exhausting dreams of trying futilely
to get who-knows-where
suffocate my ante-meridian cheer,
leaving it gasping and helpless
like a fish flopping on a pitching deck,
while a pry bar forged of need and habit,
tempered with a dash of hope,
levers me upright.

The usual ailments and aches
report for duty, along with
a couple of new recruits this time.
Preliminary ablutions, and
into the dining room,
summer vista of the yard on
full and blinding display,
when comes a tapping, a rapping
at the window feeder,
not of the fabled raven, but a
dazzling fusion of black, white and
vermilion, a male rose-breasted grosbeak
instantly joined by his streaked and tawny lady,
insistently gesturing farther out, to the
youthful red-bellied woodpecker,
scarlet head patch about to burst forth,
and the black-white medley of an
arriving downy on the squirrel buster,
and a few feet over saffron mother oriole

doting on her gawky youngster at the jelly station.
A crimson flash reveals a cardinal
lounging on the arbour,
a rusty streak signals an incoming
robin to frolic in the birdbath.

Weakness receding, weariness fading,
Onward? I ask, gazing on the avian throng;
Quoth my wingéd visitors one and all, *Evermore.*

Signs

September Sunday in my hammock,
cradled in the green bower
on the lower level,
seeking salve for today's
litany of anxieties and aches,
relief from the bleak fear
the seasons are changing too fast.
A few insect neighbours pay
their flitting compliments,
gentle breeze wafts the comforting
rasp of a distant cicada
while a squirrel chats up the
unseasonable warmth with the nearest oak.
Lady Hummingbird zips in to imbibe
of the liquid feeders and a few flowers:
she's here late this year.
A blaze of orange announces
A bigger surprise:
the Oriole family, still gracing
their summer haunts,
have dropped in to join Lady H.
Perhaps winter is a ways off yet.

Turtle

Sometimes I've spotted you
basking on a sun-drenched log,
sometimes gliding through a thriving pond,
sometimes just a silhouette on a road sign
warning you might hopefully lumber across,
and I see a familiar shell,
carapace above fused to plastron below,
weighty, mosaiced camouflage
to deceive inobservant predators,
rugged protection to frustrate
those who draw near,
and perhaps a bit of decoration,
a touch of style,
a little virtue in necessity,
a necessity become inescapable encumbrance,
slowing you to a near-crawl,
forever hiding your true shape,
an ever-present, unrelenting burden.

I see too how the world becomes
too much, or gets too close
and you pull into the refuge,
the vulnerable core feeling safe,
just the armour lying inert in the sun.

Fears abating, we tentatively
nose the air, hoist up our burdens,
and trundle stoically onward.

Portraits

The Great Wall

August, blistering hot, unseen cicadas loudly rasping,
a different buzz than at home,
crows cawing us on our way,
me with sunhat, heavy day pack,
battered little red umbrella for a parasol,
slowing down my much younger companions
as we hike the great brick snake,
up the ridge, following terrain,
our potential path reaching
as far as the eye can see into the hills.
No one around, we three alone with
the buzz and the calls, the vistas and the heat,
The Wall and our reflections.

Centuries old, origins of its mostly vanished
predecessor more than two millennia in the past,
stretching through the ancient country
an imponderable distance, built to keep
the future invader, to keep chaos, out.
The power, the audacity to order it built,
the commitment, the subservience to translate
command into hard reality.
For a time, a bulwark against the outside,
but long since overrun, a reminder
that all control, all rule, no matter
how fearsome or fixed-seeming, is, in the end,
fleeting, an eddy in the great river of history.

Some parts now the domain of tourists,
others abandoned to the crows and cicadas,
and the ghosts of the tens, hundreds of thousands
who died bringing it all about
silently alongside as we climb and marvel.

Not a border or barrier anymore,
but now a part of the spectacular scenery,
somehow enhancing the natural, setting it off.
Construction's contemporaneous
temporal power now superseded,
but the vision, the achievement,
the sacrifice, the lessons, remain.

The Oaks

For three decades surveying my little domain
you have always been there, on the lower level,
twins soaring majestically at the back of the yard,
full leaf in summer conferring cooling shade,
glowing bronze in autumn, last to give up your leaves,
bending but holding fast through winter's storms,
spring budding bringing hope of renewal,
home to squirrels and bird-friends,
reaching far down and drinking deeply from Mother Earth,
stretching sunward and spreading out
imperceptibly day by day, but boldly from year to year,
exuding life-giving oxygen.
Scouting abodes back then, the moment I saw you
I knew this was where I wanted to be, where I had to be;
After thirty years, do you sense my flitting presence?
Somehow I think you do; certainly I feel yours
when I breathe and slow down.

Rightmost, just this side of the shed,
gloriously powerful and symmetrical,
gantry for feeders and our rope swing,
anchor for the whole area;
Leftmost, in the corner—we worked through
your bracket fungus, me following healing instructions,
you patiently sealing shut the gap;
Skewed left up high, perhaps a pruning scar writ large,
not as harmonious as your companion, but a
rugged beauty all your own.

Well over a century and a half ago
two acorns germinated, giving birth far away
from the then town of London, Canada West,
and outside the little village of Byron,

on traditional Indigenous lands;
Now two giants engulfed by a subdivision,
yet you stand strong and proud,
living testimony to a once vast primeval forest whose
ghosts are all around, on the twilight edge of perception.
Let us three bear witness to it together;
May its spirit and descendants
grace and heal our land.

Swing

For Rheta and Ray

The band kicks off an old, familiar tune,
and across the hall I see both rise, slowly,
time-worn joints and limbs creakily obeying,
and shuffle out onto the dance space.
They respond to the beat, hesitatingly,
but soon the rhythms and chords
from a vanished era cast their spell;
evident joy in memory,
in the moment and each other,
reawakened movements gracefully merge and flow,
the decades dissipate, time's illusion melts away,
revealing a duet, now, and always,
forever young and in love.

In Memory of Claudius Cossus

The lines from Tacitus are few, but packed with meaning,
colourful detail illuminating a portrait of chaos
bequeathed by Nero`s downfall and suicide,
a time the Roman Imperium tottered and tore itself apart.

The year of four emperors, Vitellius, number three,
marching on Rome with his German legions to
briefly grasp the laurel wreath before it slipped away and
momentarily don the purple before it was violently encarmined,
found his triumphal progress unrecognized and unwanted
in the land of the Helvetii.

Swiftly crushing the Swiss forebears he descended on Aventicum,
their surrendering capital, executed out of hand the
ostensible revolt leader, and paused to imbibe the unslaked
bloodlust of his legionaries braying for rape, pillage and slaughter.

The town's pleading delegation quailed
under Vitellius' bluster and threats
when came forward Claudius Cossus,
        nervous but undaunted,
        learning his shield,
        eloquence his blade,
        this time his destiny.

Memories of that extraordinary day now reside
in a few words of an aristocratic Empire annalist,
sole testimony to the flights of oratorical emotion
that soared over the sea of swords, spears and bows
fresh from butchery and quivering for more,
the language of mercy holding fast
against the demons of destruction,
building a bridge of humanity over a chasm of hatred,

bristling host rendered passionately compassionate,
in turn binding Vitellius' twitching hand.

The ruins outside Avenches are peaceful now,
most from the later, centuries-long
Pax Romana of prosperity and subjugation,
some articulate ethereal echoes bouncing
amongst scattered stones, mute witnesses to the
magnificent moment when one solitary soul
stepped up, spoke peace, forestalled an army
and saved a city.

Marcus

A sharp nip in the air this morning,
a whisper on the breeze
that winter is stealing in,
first snowfall just behind.
For thirteen seasons past
you romped through it,
each time like it was the first.
This year, the snow will remain
trackless, the yard quiet.
I gaze now on the still-green lawn,
your chasms filled in and grown over,
my unwanted victory.

I see you as a puppy,
pointer-sized and too big, too rambunctious,
not what we were looking for,
but what we were fated
to find. An independent, noble soul,
you knew your own mind,
carved out your space,
liberally donated white hair to all surfaces,
took over the futon,
contentedly dozing while
we gathered round the screen.

Ah, but outdoors was your true home,
charging after squirrels and chipmunks
(executing a few laggards),
digging up moles, warning off dogs and cats,
peering through the great cedar hedge
with your one good eye,
insisting on your walks.
And oh how you loved them!

In all seasons transformed, ecstatically alive--
summer's enveloping heat, fall's crisp chill,
fresh dewy air after spring showers,
all such an incredible joy to you.
Even winter, biting cold,
driving sleet hurling ears
straight back, you simply leaned in
and forged happily on, complaining human
struggling in your wake.
Only rain sent you slinking back
to couch and hearth.

After more than a decade, portents,
straws in the wind—
sound retreating from your world,
proud autonomy metamorphosing
into affectionate dependence,
sleeping right outside the bedroom door,
slowing pace, refusing food;
and, inevitably, diagnosis: an internal invader,
you shouldn't even be alive.
But how you fought on,
defied them all, stayed true,
even on that final morning insisting
on one last staggering sniff around your domain,
consecrated since with your ashes;
our favourite trail too.

And now, the wind has changed,
the seasons shifting yet again.
Look, it's snowing! Go on, Marcus.

Carmanah Walbran

Some years ago now we journeyed
to Vancouver Island.
This will be great! said Graham,
who lived in Vancouver,
*while you're here you have
to see Carmanah Walbran.
It's one of the few patches
of old growth rainforest left
on the island. It's very special.
Come the weekend I'll cross
over from the mainland;
we can meet up at
my brother-in-law Paul's
country place and go
from there.* Caught up in
his enthusiasm, we
(Andrew, Donna and I) agreed.

And so it came to pass.
Enjoy, said Paul, *I'll have
a barbecue ready when you
return.* And so we
bounced and jolted more than
two hours on a logging road
filled with ruts and craters
big enough, it looked, to swallow
the van, or least take off a wheel,
pausing only to rest our labouring
vehicle (and the driver) at a spectacular
view that suddenly presented itself.
Onward we forged, and then,
finally, but suddenly, we were there,
the Welcome sign marking the

gravel parking lot at the destination.

Alighting, we entered the domain
of the ancient forest giants,
towering majestically overhead,
moss everywhere, clinging to
the massive trunks, hanging
from branches. For sound,
our footsteps, the occasional
bird, the murmuring stream
when we were near it, the
gentle roaring of the waterfall
in the distance,
and our attempted
expressions of awe.

For there was more here
than a family of gentle titans.
We were embraced by a wave
whose origins seemed
lost in time, and from some
other dimension entirely.
We all felt it; *It's like there's
a wisdom coming out of the
trees* declared Graham; Paul later
said simply *It's a very spiritual place*.
Andrew and Donna wandered, in wonder.
As for me, I tried to find the words,
but didn't, really. I only knew,
instinctively, that it was a place
where the material universe parts a bit,
opening a doorway. It brought back
a memory from another place,
far away, and from another time.
All too soon we reached the hour
to leave the sacred space.

We bounced and jolted
our way out, blowing a tire
on the way, back to the barbecue,
to the rest of the trip, to the rest
of our life journeys, but changed,
maybe a bit, maybe profoundly.

Soaring Sitka spruce,
the largest impossibly high,
magnificent Douglas fir,
enormous red cedars that
have seen a millennium of
rain and sun come and go;
will we have the wisdom to
let your realm remain, in peace,
for generations unborn to
rediscover, to feel in their turn
the kinship, the embrace,
to find anew that doorway and
the connection.

Hypostyle Hall

A memory pegged to my wall,
enlivening an intimate space,
passed by thousands of times,
until suddenly pulled in,
pulled back over thirty years
into the July desert heat.

Floating Nile hotel taking rest
at fabled Karnak, marvelling visitors
disgorged to stroll goggle-eyed
through prodigious monumentality,
engulfing conglomeration of
temples, chapels, pylons, stelae.
Origins three millennia past,
mutated through thirty pharaonic reigns,
abandoned after twenty centuries to
temporary Christian repurposing,
now roofless, partly tumbled away,
embracing sun, wind, sand and tourists.

Enfolded by the Hypostyle Hall,
dizzying testament, vast forest of
immense inscribed pillars soaring skywards,
on the hunt for a photogenic angle to
imprison everything around with one image,
and there, in the distance through a channel
in the maze towards the light,
a white heat-reflecting shirt,
one lone figure perched on a base
between stints guiding for baksheesh,
seemingly dwarfed but the beating heart.

Exultant, I raise my camera, focus, and click.

Remembrance Day 2017

Damp cold, yesterday's snow sublimating,
iron-grey sky, with an intimation of sun behind,
many hearts beating behind a poppy,
some select chests nobly bemedalled,
still gleaming in the muted light.
Spirits command aging bodies that,
remembering youth and strength,
pull to attention.

Last Post's lament weaving around and beyond
Cathedral bells tolling eleven,
time marching, but suspended
for a respectful moment.
Blanket of silence descends,
just a stray thread of restless childhood here and there,
the air thick with memory,
with pride and pain, comradeship and loss.
Names to some, past reality present
once again to a few, float by:
Kandahar, Kapyong, Hill 355;
Dieppe, the Atlantic, Bomber Command;
Ortona, D-Day, the Scheldt.
Others, now bereft of living memory,
are nonetheless here:
Ypres, Vimy, Passchendaele, Amiens.

Ceremony's end approaches;
our turn comes, we lay a wreath,
and pause, arm in arm,
trying, but not able, to imagine,
sorrow and gratitude and marvelling respect
flowing together, holding aloft that torch
thrown from other hands.

Limoncocha Rainforest

Leaving behind oil fields
and shanty town,
past the coffee cooperative,
off the end of the road,
into a motorized dugout
and mooring alongside our
overgrown houseboat.
Cast off, floating down the Napo's
tropical waters destined
for the mighty Amazon,
floating past the river flat used
by the crew for a soccer pitch,
floating to the sounds of the Andes
brought to the lowlands
by the boat's company.

Vacating our vessel's womb,
quick baptism amongst
incurious piranhas,
and into the embracing foliage,
into a heart, but not of darkness.
Stumbling behind Jaime and his machete
reopening the barely discernible path,
caressed by dangling vines,
homage paid to forest elders,
soaring, sheltering kapok trees.
In the canopy above
roaring howler monkeys
and flitting birds of every hue and call;
in the tangle below
columns of army ants march off to war,
leaf-cutters make off with outsize loads,
tree frogs ogle the outsiders,

black and scarlet assassin bugs
hunt through the undergrowth,
hand-sized snails ooze along underfoot.

Sun slipping away, we diurnal humans
retreat to our river-borne den,
caimans patrol the lagoon,
eyes mirroring any flashlight's probe,
night monkeys let loose with
grunts, screams, moans and hoots,
nocturnal insects issue forth to
click, whirr and trill,
owls and currasows take wing
and swell the chorus.

Ancient forest here once decimated,
but land abandoned to
questing, restless, relentless life,
     high and low,
     loud and silent,
     fleeting and enduring,
life searching within, recalling the wonder,
life reaching out in collective resurrection
of the memory.

Bluesman

For James Cotton

Fryfogle's it was called,
on the south side of Dundas,
just west of Wellington,
a little spot that back around
the mid-eighties drew some
big acts for those in the know,
sometimes jamming the place
way beyond fire code.
I was young back then, early twenties,
Caucasian-Canadian university student,
time stretching in front of me like
an endless-seeming ocean.
Read that somebody called
James Cotton was coming to Fry's,
a mean harmonica player,
an ace purveyor of the Blues, foundation
for much of what we listened to.
I'd never paid attention to that
but was looking to fill an evening,
was ready to give a hearing,
slid on down early, staked out
a primo spot, stage-side table,
and cued up a beverage.

Born eighth of eight to
African-American sharecroppers,
poor Delta country near Tunica Mississippi,
forty miles south of fabled Memphis.
Papa Mose doubled as a Baptist preacher,
Mama Hattie loved playing harmonica.
Learned the harp from her quickly
while still Mozart-young,

entertaining field hands, blazing away
at Saturday night juke joints.
Orphaned at nine, your well-named Uncle Wiley,
bound and determined all that talent
would not be wasted on cotton fields and
small-time joints, wangled an intro
to a harp master, the second
Sonny Boy Williamson, Rice Miller.
The scheme worked, he took you in,
handed on the secrets,
passed down the traditions,
showed you life on the road,
until he had to follow a different star,
left you, at fifteen, his band.
Too immature, too wild and crazy, it all splintered.
Kept playing and kicking around until
Destiny stepped in and hooked you up
with the legendary Muddy Waters
as a backup plan for the
brilliant, tormented Little Walter.
By 1960 you were Muddy's main man,
spectacularly breaking out at the
Newport Jazz Festival.
By '66 fronting your own group and
on the long, meandering road to London, Ontario.

Roots stretching all the way to Africa,
nurtured and brought to bloom by
descendants of slaves in the Deep South
welding spirituals and work songs,
hardscrabble striving and fierce passion,
theoretically uncomplicated
yet technically deceptive
and viscerally a cathartic,
musical Mount Everest
encompassing despair and hope,

love and heartbreak, all of life,
scaled only by the intrepid
gifted with ropes of
imagination and creativity
hooked to pitons of
deep feeling and honesty,
including the Delta son of
an amateur player and a preacher.

You bounced out on stage with the band,
launched into the first number,
a firestorm of radiant joy in the moment,
energy enough to power the street,
enveloping the room with a
scintillating tonal mosaic,
voice rich as pecan pie,
harmonica an extension of the soul,
pulling sounds unearthly and deep-rooted,
stinging and caressing, moulded
into a majestic emotional bridge
spanning one and all.
But it was the eyes, mirroring every note,
looking right inside and pulling me in,
linking across age, culture, heritage,
leaving a mark indelible and
a lifelong love affair with the music.

The Central Library occupies the space now,
drawing children to explore,
workers to lunch in the reading garden,
concert-goers to the Wolf Hall,
street folk looking for shelter for a while,
the curious to hunt up a book
or search out a website,
CBC Radio to their new storefront home;
but there will always be an intimate bar,

a young student from the north,
and a Blues master blowing down barriers
and bidding eloquent, exuberant welcome.

Notre-Dame is Burning

Notre-Dame is burning,
so the news says. Here,
a radiant blue dazzles from above,
crisp, chill midday air cradling the
promise of vernal renewal;
An ocean away acrid, sallow plumes
churn skyward, first flickers of flaming
roof animating the early evening.

Notre-Dame is burning.
My adolescent avatar was there
thirty-seven years ago, passed through
the overpowering Gothic façade
from bustling streets and glaring sun to
hallowed hush and glimmering
devotional candles,
gawped at the great rose windows
iridescing the morning light,
trooped with the other ogling tourists
around the adamantine immensity.

Notre-Dame is burning
the breathless reports
and looping videos
flash around the world,
a modest miracle of timing
in the fallow between
Palm Sunday and Maundy Thursday.

Notre-Dame is burning,
and already the question: how?
and already the speculation:
renovations gone disastrously awry,

some electrical fault, or maybe
a carelessly flung cigarette butt.

Notre-Dame is burning.
Conceived in 1160, two hundred years
in gestation, a monumental
gesture of hope and faith,
awesome architectural heirloom,
witness to a vast historical pageant,
gazing impassively through the centuries
on the wealthy few and
the innumerable misérables,
time's shifting tides accreting onto
the spiritual symbol many other meanings.

Notre-Dame is burning
overhead while first responders,
priests and specialists rush to remove
and pack and desperately pass
glorious art and priceless artefacts
down a human chain and out to safety.

Notre-Dame is burning,
great jets of triumphant fire
streaking heavenward
split the gathering dark,
grotesque smoky billows
metastasize from white to orange
to yellow to green to glowering black
under the horrified stares
of a growing flock praying,
singing, filming, despairing,
hoping, stunned at the sight
of their pride and joy,
an ecclesiastical masterpiece become
heart of a secular nation,

being ripped out and incinerated.

Notre-Dame is burning,
the nineteenth century spire
become soaring torch, then
plummeting into the raging inferno
engulfing the timber-forested crown.

Notre-Dame is burning,
survivor of endless religious conflicts,
desecration,
revolution,
hundreds of years of neglect,
the agonies of two World Wars,
its shocking dénouement seemingly
suddenly at hand.

Notre-Dame is burning,
and where would Quasimodo be?
I wondered. No doubt guarding the
precious bells, haunting the hundreds
of firefighters pouring on water from
far below and making a stand
in the twin towers,
defying destruction's fiery grasp.

Notre-Dame is burning,
but the conflagration is fading,
the inestimable roof beams logged
from trees long-gone from France
now a pile of ash, yet the
life's work of uncounted medieval
stonemasons still standing strong,
their shades shoulder-to-shoulder
with those wielding the hoses.

Notre-Dame is burning,
gently, but searching lights reveal
the wondrous stained glass
still intact as well,
the famous organ wounded
but a survivor too,
those candles flickering on.

Notre-Dame was burning,
but will, it is vowed,
be gloriously renaissant,
fortunes formerly withheld
suddenly free to re-form
and reimagine the individual,
collective and digital memory,
meld modern with Middle Ages,
defying time and history's edict
that all things must pass.

Notre-Dame was burning,
but now is calling for me to return,
this time not to pay homage
to a frozen monument,
but to bask in a living metamorphosis,
to feel it all happen again,
twenty-first century craftsmen imbued
with the spirits of their distant ancestors,
mortality breaking bonds and
striving upwards to touch
immortality.

Mission: Impossible—Squirrel Protocol

With apologies to the Mission: Impossible
movie franchise

Two decades ago I plotted and planned,
how to give my wingéd friends
a mammal-free feed station,
near enough so we could commune,
far enough for feathered comfort.
Picked the spot carefully,
laid pebbled paving stones to
catch seed fall, encouraging
four-legged creatures to stay ground-bound;
extended the pole higher than leaping height;
cut back Olive, the ancient oak,
to eliminate overhead access;
experimented to find just the right
baffle to defeat climbers.
Year in and out I gazed on smugly,
birds on the feeder, squirrels and their ilk
scampering on the lawn or skittering
along too-distant branches;
all was right with the world.

Then, one day, there you were,
black squirrel, lounging on the hopper
and gorging contentedly on forbidden seed.
Aghast I banged the window,
chased you off and wondered, how?
Months floated by, more sightings and bangings,
knowing it was just you, my furry nemesis,
your method never spotted.

Come a winter afternoon, the ritual repeated,
but something about your comportment

caught my eye, and I mounted a stakeout.
Up the arbor, onto a convenient oak branch,
back to the trunk, return along another limb,
tiptoe onto a twig, and
Flung
out and down, an arboreal Ethan Hunt,
in true Mission: Impossible fashion all
the plotting and planning culminating in a
daring flying leap, limbs splayed,
riding the air, and plop, claws gripping
the feeder's snowy roof, and then
hop down to indulge once again.
Squirrel, I salute you.

And so, the key was treachery.
Betrayed by Olive, year in and out
slowly, slowly, extending a precarious launch pad.
But why?
Sympathy for your little friend?
Revenge for pruning?
We will have to confer.

And now, my choice—
Prune back, re-establish dominance?
or accommodate your occasional
triumphant forays?
I will mull it over.

Linda

A response to the bronze statue Linda
by Elizabeth Wyn Wood

Far have I come and
here I stand, my path
unfolding before me.

Here I begin anew,
flowing from Mother Earth
and ready to take wing.

Here I am, see me now
manifest, unfettered
and free.

East Wind

To Dad

Born in the realms of sunrise,
maturing over Buffalo,
gathering strength as it rolls
westward down Erie,
hurtling through the Nanticoke-Long Point gap,
bursting forth an elemental symphony
onto our waiting shore.
Pleasure craft confined to safe harbours,
trees bent and strained, planters blown over,
whitecaps foaming in the distance,
breakers far past the second sandbar
flinging skyward thrill-seeking kitesurfers
and roiling up sand and seaweed
to hurl ashore.
Swept up in the middle of a
traditional three day blow
I stand out on the rocks
near the crashing waves,
hair streamed back, leaning in like a
mermaid on the prow of a clipper.
Beachgoers chased away,
except for the kitesurfers and
a few hardy souls who share the secret,
likewise alive in the moment,
a knowing smile, an understanding wave,
conversation beyond an arm's-length
drowned by the din.

And back there, on the bench swing
tucked into the corner of the yard,
ensconced where Mom bundled him up,
is Dad, determined to be here,

determined to face the gale,
grass just to his front a tiny green swirling ocean,
bamboo to the right whipped into a frenzy,
watching seagulls beating against the tempest,
now hovering in place, now gaining precious metres.
Old Man Willow across the little road,
ancient shore sentinel, hangs on, for now;
Mary's silver maple on the other side
of the dirt drive just a memory.
And churned up with the sediment
other memories, long ago warm summer gales,
us kids exhilarated body surfers,
flying like marlins through the shallows,
Grampy scanning with binoculars
for the big Lakers that bounce on the horizon,
driven closer from open water
to hew a safer course.

On this chill fall day Nature's chorale
thunders through and around us,
steady with enervating crescendos,
lifting up all who spread their wings
and brave the east wind.

Barnardo Boy

*To my grandfather, Harold Mays Wenn, and the
many others, whether named or not, who came
into his story or my search;
and to all of the other Home Children*

Prologue

Embark on a family epic,
two entwined tales.

One, a saga rooted in
northeast England:
Two principle poles,
the fishing ports of Yarmouth
and, farther north, Grimsby;
A saga rooted in a love story,
in two humble working people,
Albert and Molly:
Albert, Grimsby fisherman
close to his parents and his sons;
Molly, Yarmouth housewife turned
herring splitter seeking work
in the north;
The saga branching into a
love child, my grandfather Harold,
and his adoption that brought
Harold to a new family,
and later an extraordinary voyage;
That same adoption sending
Albert and Molly
on a separate course.

The other tale is a quest
for solutions to mysteries:
A young teen bereft of a grandfather

(who had brought much humour
but no family history)
in search of the man lost
and never truly known,
asking questions not posed to him,
seeking answers, some he had
many he never knew,
the hunt stretching over
four decades as I followed
my own journey into middle age
and across the gender divide
from male to female,
from Jeff to Jennifer,
always looking for certainty,
looking for stories,
looking to morph Barnardo Boy
from a mark of shame
to a badge of distinction,
determined to honour him
and the entire family,
passed on and living,
that was waiting for me.

Two formidable strands
winding and weaving
together across time and space.

1
Carefully preserved aging snapshots
in my mental photo album,
exuding still-poignant life and meaning:
A tall, laughing presence, Grandpa to me,
open face and ostentatious nose,
social partner in his household;
Raking leaves for leaping grandchildren;

Fishing with buddies and family,
then happily and masterfully filleting
when all others demurred;
Gleefully sharing Andy Capp,
lovable comic strip layabout
reawakening northeast English
childhood memories.
Just once did the eyes cloud
and the gleam waver,
a silly quiz inflaming painful
memories of an education denied.
Turning the page, glancing up,
finding a sunset stealing in.

2

A tale of two towns, Yarmouth the first,
east coast mouth of the River Yare,
an island transformed to peninsula
paralleling the North Sea,
straddling Norfolk and Suffolk; and
straddling economies old and new.
Herring port for a millennium, foremost
in England, celebrated with a six week fair.
Object of Dickensian affection,
town and tide mixed up like toast and water,
perfumed with *fish and pitch and oakum and tar,*
narrow lanes echoing with the
thwack of shipwrights and clang of forges,
and, soaring above all, the great Church of St. Nicholas,
which saw the trawler boom come
then go when the railway opened up
thrusting Grimsby closer to the fishing grounds,
which gazed on as early tourists discovered
Yarmouth`s seaside charms.
Dangling just over the River Bure

forty-four acres of land and three of water
known as Runham Vauxhall,
home to manure works, fish offices, lower rates,
and Molly, with baby Freddy and a husband
fighting consumption`s onset,
her need for a job answered by a helping hand
from family friends to the north;
And so, leaving husband and child
with in-laws, she found herself in 1908
alone on the road to bustling Grimsby.

Founded by Grim, a ninth century
shipwrecked Dane, first dwelling
fashioned from his vessel`s remains,
first fishing port in England,
after three hundred years
forced into centuries of hibernation
by a silted harbour.
Then came the magical nineteenth century,
harbour reborn, a railroad lifeline,
huge new fish landing pontoons,
twenty-three acres of docks,
a meteoric rise ensuing, plateau
and slow decline over the horizon.
Airy, yet plagued with rising sewage
when the tide was in,
to some eyes clean and boasting a lovely park,
to others a sullied jumble of hovels, prosperous homes,
timber yards and a welter of shops;
Workaday, focussed on the port boasting
a mile-long covered roof,
the largest fish market in the world
serving a hundred trawlers at once,
redolent of tons of fresh catch,
ringing with the auctioneers' cries;
Home to Henry Mays' fish factory, Molly's destination;

Home to Albert, trawlerman and dock worker,
scion of the Mays family with two sons,
young Harry and little Albert Junior,
and an estranged wife;
Site of a fateful, destined encounter.

3
Moment indelible, like
a butterfly trapped in amber,
first year of high school,
twelve days before Christmas,
unexpectedly picked up,
disbelieving Dad's tearful revelation
that Grandpa was taken
just today, his heart, sudden
but a known issue,
the imago imbued with
heightened poignancy
by the season and Grandpa's
just completed family present,
a hand-built doghouse for Rags.

Turning inward, I confronted
a gaping, grief-stained,
laughter-sized hole opening up.

4
Observe a working couple,
Henry and Eleanor Mays, and their
modest Grimsby house, Eleanor's charge,
not far from docks and Henry's establishment,
home also to their son Albert (when onshore),
Albert's three siblings and his two little boys.
Observe this bustling household
welcome a new guest, Molly,

Eleanor's friend across a generation,
come from Yarmouth to be a herring splitter:
Gut and cut close down the backbone,
preserve the skin to keep it in one piece,
thread through the gill onto the
spreet for the smokehouse,
fast, precise, painstaking, twelve hours a day,
some extra on Saturday;
The money good, desires seemingly achieved.

Out beyond the played-out North Sea
an early steam trawler, held together by
cement, iron-rust and God's will,
heaves up and hammers down,
Albert and the rest wind out
a thousand fathoms or more
of steel warp towing the trawl
and steam-winch it back to unload
the whitefish catch scraped off the bottom,
day in and out to fill the hold;
Arduous, demanding, well-paid,
hazard lurking in every wave,
but Albert fully alive,
or so he thought.

Came the day when Molly beheld
on the threshold, sandy-haired,
proudly bearing the Mays nose,
twinkling eyes and a knowing smile,
an unknowingly long-awaited figure,
freshly released by the deep waters;
Came the day when Albert beheld
the Mays' new boarder,
quite tall, medium-dark hair,
not conventionally pretty but
alight with a humour and fire that

glowed around her smile's corners,
an answer to an unasked question;
Came the day when embers blazed forth,
consuming consideration and duty,
consuming convention, expectation and practicality,
roaring on despite spouses and children,
despite a shared, crowded abode,
enduring a consequently chilled friendship,
enduring little Albert Junior's tragic passing,
melded and fused into a burgeoning new life,
incarnated September 14, 1909,
a new life named Harold Mays Wenn.

Hovering in the birth room
unbanished ghosts: duty,
practicality, convention, expectation,
spectres given full-throated voice
by Henry and Eleanor and only cast out
by a haunting, momentous decision.
The verdict? Shatter the nascent family:
Albert once more into the arms of the ocean;
Molly back to beckoning Yarmouth;
Baby Harold and a sacred mission
entrusted to friends through the Grimsby fishery,
entrusted to Susannah and Frederick,
living three-quarters of a mile away by foot,
other side of the Haven waterway
now become a gaping chasm.

5
Grappling with a loss, the first
to consciously touch my spirit,
reflecting on others gone before him,
the traditions handed down,
forebears and bygone days remembered,

family trees shown and explained,
stories passed on,
all eagerly soaked up by
my history-loving soul.

But now, reflecting on Grandpa—
a frustrating lacuna,
the past shrouded in silence,
only the shadows of a hidden canvas,
a lifelong sense that one shouldn't ask,
a sense now beaten back and routed by
an assault of youthful determination and
vanity that the river of oblivion could be bridged,
the desperately unlikely achieved
and the blanks painted in,
family and history re-found,
his presence re-imagined
and memory honoured;
This assault launched by my thirst
for comfort in mysteries solved,
driven onward by my embryonic
hunger for meaning.

6

Water proving thicker than blood,
forever sundered from birth parents,
a little Odysseus, with flavourings of
David Copperfield and Oliver Twist,
sets out. Scenes from the voyage:
     New Mom Susannah, daughter of a fisherman
     who crewed a vessel that vanished at sea,
     Susannah always there, bringing along
     all those aunts and uncles and cousins.
     The little adopted one renamed Freddie Hansen
     after new Dad, an immigrant from the

wild Faroe Islands, likewise living off the sea.
A happy time in Grimsby, but look again at the picture,
age three, the pensive expression, eyes
searching for an incoming storm.
[...]
You're not yet four, this will be hard,
but Dad's not coming home,
he's sleeping deep in the sea.
I guess you won't remember him much.
We'll manage somehow.
[...]
It's been two years, and now I have
something to tell you. You remember
Uncle George Boyce? He's your new Dad,
so we're going to start calling you Freddie Boyce.
He was a fisherman too but he's become a soldier.
And your big cousin Edie is now your sister.
[...]
Come closer. I am not well, and soon
will be gone, consumption is taking me.
Your Dad George is still at war,
Edie's married now, but she and
the rest of the family don't have
money to feed an extra mouth,
so I've arranged for you to be looked after
by an orphanage called Dr. Barnardo's Homes.
They're a good Christian organization,
the biggest and one of the oldest in the country.
You're nearly nine now, I know you will
be a brave boy.
[...]
Welcome to Dr. Barnardo's Homes.
We are truly, sincerely sorry about
your Mom Susannah; she fought
the tuberculosis as long as she could.
I can see you're scared, but we

are your family now. Come,
we would like to take a picture
for our records; you look really
handsome in your sweater and
bow tie. By the way, we have
to call you by your birth name,
Harold Wenn.
[...]
You've been at our Clapham Home
in London, our musical centre,
nearly two years now, and
you are getting too old to be here.
We wanted to send you to Canada,
but your stepsister Edie hopes
she can take you in some day.
So now we are going to send you to
a nice foster family near Birmingham.
[...]
Well, you weren't long up north.
We have brought you from Birmingham
here to our Boys Garden City because
we are concerned about your health.
You may even have contracted
tb as well, so we are soon
passing you on to Teighmore House,
on Jersey Island. Nothing like
bracing sea breezes.
[...]
Hoy mate, welcome to Jersey!
Lovely place this, but don't
be fooled. You've been around,
know the drill, we're numbers more
than boys, like every other place it's
a bloody military camp, up early,
lots of clean and tidy, school naturally,
and of course you know how they love

*to bark the Bible at you. But
watch out, they can be absolute beasts
out here, beat one of us to death for
stealing a tomato. But if you keep
your head down you'll be ok, might get
a little farm training, we
got us a private beach to swim in
Grauville Bay, and the air
is the cleanest anywhere.
[...]
Welcome back to the Boys Garden City
on this February day in 1921. You seem
to have thrived out there and your stepsister
has stepped back, so we have good news:
You sail for Canada on March 17!
You won't be truly alone, over 100
other boys and girls and Mr. Hobday himself,
our representative in Canada, are sailing too.
You'll be placed on a farm and I know you
will do all you can to give them satisfaction.
Here's a New Testament with lots of marked-off
inspirational passages. And a nice metal trunk
to pack your things in. Bon voyage.
[...]
This is the SS Scandinavian, an old ship but
a good one. Harold, I see you have a
large dent in your trunk lid; jumped on it
trying to close it, I understand.
Your daily routine here will begin with
rising at 6am to go through the wash house,
then line up again for breakfast. The dining hall,
you'll find, is appointed with long wooden
tables and benches. In ten days we dock
at St. John, New Brunswick. You'll be up
at 5am that day to march on deck and claim
your trunk, following which you will disembark*

for a medical inspection before heading to Toronto.
[...]
I hope the rail journey was alright, it's a long one,
more than a day and a half. It's now past midnight
and we will go straight to our headquarters.
Your guardians will be Mr. and Mrs. Wardell,
farmers near Otterville in south-western Ontario.
In five days we will send your trunk to the nearest
railway station. You will follow the next day.
I am sure you will do all you can so that they will
be proud to have you in their home.
I want you to go to Church and Sunday School
regularly and so live as to maintain the
good name of Dr. Barnardo's Homes and
honour our living heavenly Father.
[...]
Hello, Harold, I am Mr. Wardell. We were expecting
an 18 year old, which you, just a boy, clearly are not.
You are staying with us over the weekend, and
we will return you on Monday. In the meantime,
the moment we get to the farm I will have you
plow a field with my team of three horses.
Never done that? You'll learn quick enough.
[...]
Good news, we have decided to keep you after all.

And thus, two new fathers while still young
and then, in a scant two and half years,
from a loving home in an English port
to being ostensibly orphaned and an indentured
eleven-year old servant on a Canadian farm.

7
First tentative conversations with
Grandma Wenn and Dad,

first mention of Barnardo's,
perusing old letters from someone named Edie,
     sorry we couldn't take you in,
     may your life there turn out well
and much later
     nice to reconnect, looking forward to your visit.
Harold's birth certificate with no father listed,
just that odd middle name Mays.
A reply from Barnardo's—he was
adopted at birth, a sketch of his journey through
orphanages to the promised land of Canada.

All of us to England in 1981, noting relevant-looking
names and their addresses from phonebooks;
Hoisting giant bound volumes on and off shelves
at the General Register Office, looking for
index entries to birth, death and marriage
certificates connected to Harold,
two hours of heaving up and down just to find
mother Molly's death reference from 1973;
Dad and I to Barnardo's, Grandpa's file
carefully concealed, scraps of information
tossed out if the right question asked.

Home again, sitting with Mom and Dad and Granny Seaton,
addressing letter after hopeful letter to those names,
replies drifting in, many best wishes,
a new pen-pal in elderly Jack, a couple of faint hints.

Certificates arrive, some tangible clues, and
Dad's idea:
     Try a long-shot, write to the address where Molly died;
     Yes, it's been eight years since she passed on,
     but you never know.
The whole patchy, embryonic story
packaged up and posted, provoking,

some weeks later, an epistolary thunderbolt:
>*Yes, Molly died in our home;*
>*No, we never knew Harold existed;*
>*But yes, we are all one family—*
>*his roots, your roots, lie here.*

8

Follow now, back to 1909 England,
tumultuous autumn turning to dreary winter,
where other journeys unwind.
Watch Albert and Molly,
never married and now forced apart
say goodbye to their son,
baby Harold, their firstborn.
Follow Albert back to the trawlers,
toddler Harry left with his Grandma Eleanor,
to school early and for a time given sweets
at the gates by a mysterious motherly figure,
a woman undivorced from Albert,
the expense huge for working people
like him hauling a living
from the whitefish grounds.

Follow Molly back to Yarmouth's hurly-burly,
to declining husband Angel Wenn and to son Freddy,
back to duty, convention and expectation;
follow as Molly confronts her own
storm-tossed voyage:
>*Congratulations, it's a girl. And her name?*
>*Rhoda, lovely name.*
>*[...]*
>*Sorry your husband Angel's consumption*
>*took a turn for the worse, but as he can't*
>*earn a proper living now, the workhouse*
>*is the best place for him.*

[…]
Unfortunately Freddy seems to have
been infected by tb as well. Happily,
we've stabilised him, but I'm not sure
of the long-term prognosis.
[…]
My sincere condolences, we did our best
for little Rhoda but consumption took her,
and only a year and a half old too.
[…]
My son, Angel, your husband, is dying.
We will take him out of the
workhouse and I will care for him,
while you earn a living for yourself and Freddy.
[…]
Thank you Mrs. Wenn, that completes the
payment for your husband's funeral.
Our condolences.

Bountiful, exciting Yarmouth was now barren,
but into the ghostly silence chimed heart's call:
Grimsby, Albert's town, sent its siren song to Molly,
irresistible and overpowering, love released
to take wing and soar over conformity,
romance resumed, blended household established,
Albert switching to wartime service
in the Merchant Marine, and
in two short years Mr. and Mrs. Mays,
as the neighbours thought them, were
expecting a sibling for Harry and Freddy.

It's a girl, Molly, but, and I'm truly sorry,
there's something dreadfully wrong with her;
Best let her go.
[…]
Full name to be Alberta Mays Wenn? I see.

Only way to legally work Mays into it,
no doubt, you and her father
not being actually married.
[…]
Yes, I know you got her breathing yourself, but
it's clear now tiny Bertha, as you're calling her,
is quadriplegic. Put her in the back room,
lock the door, and forget her.
[…]
Mrs. Mays, you were horrified, I remember, and
Mr. Mays, you said "No, we won't do that."
All very noble, but additionally she likely will never speak,
is epileptic for now, and needs to be turned twice each night.
And Mr. Mays, you are away a lot. Congratulations
by the way on your commendation for bravery;
Having that collier you serve on chased by a
German submarine must have been terrifying.
As for the tot, she will die before she's ten.

With care extraordinary, Bertha lived, despite all,
joined the first day of fall, 1918, by sister Kathy
(also a Mays Wenn), and soon thereafter an
unexpected visitor:

Good afternoon, Mrs. Wenn. Your husband may be dead,
you may be living in sin with Mr. Mays, a technically
married man, and have the neighbours fooled,
but you are still legally Mrs. Wenn, correct? A fishwoman
I understand? I am from Dr. Barnardo's Homes, and
require a private conversation. Your baby and
the little cripple may stay.
This concerns Harold, the baby boy you abandoned
nine years ago. His mother, Mrs. Boyce, has died of
tuberculosis and no one else can look after him except
our Home, but unfortunately we cannot admit him
without your signature, dear Mrs. Boyce not having
had official custody. Your lifestyle is immoral and

these two unfortunates depend on you. Mr. Mays might
be on the seas somewhere, but he is not here now, is he?
Harold has tb and no doubt will die. Do sign, just here,
so we can take care of him meantime, and also avoid
a lot of unpleasantness. Thank you, I will be on my way.

9

My pilgrim's progress soaring over an ocean,
seeking the source, finding Harry,
recipient of my letter,
Grandpa's half-brother;
Reforging links long broken,
finding family, traditions and wistful wishes:
If only Grandpa had lived long enough,
if only he had reunited with them,
Harry now never to know his brother,
Grandpa's imperfect portrait painted with
recollection and anecdote.

Then to Bertha, Grandpa's sister,
devoid of speech and movement,
energies poured into remembering,
brimming with the past,
and waiting, waiting for the right
questions, waiting to affirm or deny,
Bertha whose memory mansion
included a little alcove, a strange
visitor long ago, an absent boy
said to have tb, a piece of paper;
Bertha now telling, in her own way,
pining, in her fashion, for a brother
never seen until a picture prompted
tears.

Perusing photos with Harry,

chuckling at resemblances,
revelling in his stories, together
weaving a reunited tapestry,
planning to write and phone and visit.

And back home to build with Mom and Dad
on the treasure trove of handed-on tradition,
research continuing year in and year out,
probing archives, ordering certificates
and census returns,
following a virtual journey
beyond Albert and Molly,
deeper into the past,
more precious fragments unearthed,
rebuilding the shattered mosaic
piece by piece, discovering
East Anglian villages from
Buckenham to Worsted, and
the great regional centre,
Norwich, boasting grand
castle and cathedral,
a different church every Sunday
and a new pub every night
on offer, site also of inner
slums and twisting narrow streets;
And revealing such a family pageant:
Coppersmiths, brass-workers,
a tinsmith, a cloth weaver, a wire weaver,
a gardener, a charwoman, dressmakers;
A lady's servant whose son transited
from farm hand to maltster to
husbandman to innkeeper and
then owning a dairy farm and
hiring his own servant;
A miller who ended his days
in the workhouse;

An orphan who took to the sea,
then settled as a barge waterman
and saw two of his sons follow him;
A ship's engineer, a fishmonger,
a master fishcurer who owned a
dockside fish factory; and so many
women holding it all together.
Encountering cholera, typhus and
tuberculosis, a myriad of cancers and more;
Meeting the elderly and little ones
taken oh so soon; discovering a
distraught mother who threw herself
into a river and ended her pain;
Finding slum-dwellers and middle class,
hardship and unsung triumph;
Discovering people, people with
unheralded lives and untold stories,
presences now felt all around,
an epic saga encompassing a couple
whose love broke all the rules
and their son, sent by others to
Canada in servitude, all people
of my own unknown historical drama,
people as worthy of celebration
as any monarch, and yet uncelebrated.

This forest of connection, this family,
still then alive in Harry and Bertha and
their witness, a vast inheritance
denied to Grandpa but gifted to
the next generations, to me, and now
hovering nearby, silently
calling out in search of a voice.

10
Watch now, as
the boy signed over,
plucked from
a North Sea port,
shunted through thirty months
of orphanages and
shipped overseas to serve,
once again starts anew,
now on a southwestern Ontario farm
run by the Wardells, Ken and Leita,
across the road from the Arthur family,
all far from the sea:
>Six days off the ocean liner,
>just off the train from Toronto,
>*(without so much as a glass of water*
>observed the Arthurs),
>handed the reins to a three horse
>harrowing team, ordered into the fields,
>followed by Ken brandishing a horsewhip.
>[...]
>Well fed, a good room,
>decent clothes, Christmas presents;
>Per the law, sent to school;
>Per Barnardo's contract,
>allowed to attend Sunday School
>(courtesy of the Arthurs, actually getting there).
>[...]
>Omnipresent chores.
>Morning chores
>(then run nearly two miles to school).
>Evening chores.
>Weekend chores.
>A slight boy from England?
>No matter. He's here to work.

[...]
A moment to write a letter;
Molly and Albert proscribed,
so adoptive sister/cousin Edie
the destination.
A moment amidst a spring cold snap,
fields snuggled under a
downy, pearlescent coverlet,
a sight alien to hometown Grimsby:
There's white stuff outside,
they call it snow.
[...]
Taken under the wing of the
neighbouring Arthur family,
four kids to play with
(chores permitting),
Harold included in baseball,
swimming and skating,
Church and Sunday School,
Mom and Dad Arthur spinning a peaceful
cocoon away from the fiery Wardells.
[...]
Heading down the road
with an Arthur boy,
Harold telling about his
hair-trigger guardian,
how he can turn on you
in a flash over a trifle,
how he reaches for a thick, heavy,
leather trace designed to harness
a powerful plow-horse.
Harold's shirt lifted, the back welts
still vicious and angry.
Was this the first time?
No. Not at all.
[...]

Pulling up out front, Barnardo's Visitor,
a regular inspection; but of what, or who?
Perhaps a caring review with Harold,
probing for abuse, his welfare top of mind?
Maybe not.
Rather, is Harold a good boy,
upholding Barnardo's good name?
And if Harold complained?
Once the Visitor left, the horse trace
was waiting in the barn.
[...]
School friends murmur
amongst themselves,
elders resolutely silent:
Ken Wardell is a pillar
in the community
(notwithstanding some shouting
with Leita now and then);
Harold is just a Home Child.
[...]
Sunset, sunrise.
Harold's grade eight year ending,
innate ability breaking through,
entrance exam to grade nine passed.
Congratulations.
But now out to the field for Harold,
his master and mistress having
no further obligation to learning.
Sunset for Harold's education.
Sunrise for full-time labour
on the farm.
[...]
March 31, 1926.
Indenture's end. What now?
What options for a
sixteen-year-old Barnardo Boy

in Oxford County?
So, a change in title:
Delete indentured child;
Insert poorly paid farm hand.

11
Late-nineties regime change at Barnardo's,
jealously guarded archival treasures
now gleaming in the light of day,
1981's wispy sketch of young Harold
now suffused with some
definition and colour.

But respected and happy-seeming
was the man we knew.
How did you arrive there
from your inauguration?
A love-child, but no room at that inn,
one adoptive father vanishing into
the ocean's arms and
the next into trench duty,
adoptive mother's breath stilled
by the great white death,
deemed an orphan
(biological parents notwithstanding),
plunked into a Home,
shunted here and there,
shipped like chattel across
the Atlantic to serve;
Dispatched nearly six thousand
kilometres to, well, what?

A Home Child your label,
an emblem then best veiled;
To some, substandard at most,

Britain's trash, likely syphilitic,
certainly devoid of discipline;
To others, little ones
deserving common decency,
a hand up.

What happened in those far-off days?
What flesh on the bones of whisper
and a widow's hints to questions
unasked before she left us?
What route from thence to later,
to accomplished, quick with a laugh or joke,
grudges absent or well buried?

More byways and trails to follow:
Scattered letters;
Old diaries of an old flame;
Found journals of a future wife;
Town histories and newspapers;
Descendants' fragmentary reminiscence;
Scene-setting by locals who knew the land,
understood the people.
And now-elderly testimony patiently
waiting for the prompt to speak,
unburden long-ago but carefully
preserved memory:
The daughter of your master and mistress,
who knew the household;
Three once-children across the road,
eyewitnesses to a strange arrival,
a hair-trigger temper, back welts,
school days, daily life, maturation,
adaptation, dating, unbreakable friendship;
Your sister-in-law, part of a family who
heard the town talk but still bid welcome;
Your business partner who had reached out,

heard confidences, saw your growth and
co-built prosperity.

Another chorus of voices,
all striving to fulfill a covenant.

12
Growing.
Growing older, bigger, more confident.

Growing and connecting,
your master Ken detonating,
reaching for the horse trace,
a buddy stepping in between,
You want to hit somebody, you hit me.

Growing and pushing back,
finding resolve, dismissing fear,
finding your strength,
flattening farmer Wardell yourself
behind the barn.

Growing, and cultivating
a social circle, loving
those small-town dances,
doing your strut around the room
after you arrive.

Growing with ingenuity,
slipping out an upstairs window
to a lower roof after the farm was
quiet for the night,
down a conveniently-placed ladder,
making off with Ken's car
from its distant driveshed berth,

and returning it later.

Growing and maturing,
dating the girl across the road,
parking under a tree,
confessing a longing to get away,
to be your own master.

Growing, but losing,
the Wardells finally
having their own children,
your promised inheritance
blown away by the first
baby's cry.

Growing and saving pennies,
buying your own car,
a nifty Ford Roadster,
pride of the town.

Growing, and denied,
your marriage proposal
turned down, at least so long as
you were still at the Wardells.

Growing, but still going to the
Church Young People's Group,
meeting Laura, forming a couple,
driving her 55 miles to and from
Teacher's College in Hamilton.

Growing, and surviving,
surviving a wheel coming off
and rolling down the road
ahead of your full car;
And later surviving a lone crash on ice-slick

highways coming back from Hamilton.

Growing, and earning
Ken's respect, and regret,
being seen in a new light,
time and your perseverance
triggering belated amends.

Growing, and spying a little opening,
a modest, but longed-for upgrade
from farm hand to sharecropper,
your own place, after a fashion.

Growing, and sharing a commitment,
marrying Laura, now a teacher,
April 2, 1934, bound together
for a little nearby spot
known as Jackson's Farm.

13
Two artifacts, physical evidence:
A small, worn New Testament,
          bon voyage gift,
          200 marked-off passages;
And a dark red metal trunk,
          lid featuring a large dent;
Both imbued with lingering meaning
but lonely fragments of the tale.

Companion visuals found in precious photographs:
Albert's sly twinkling grin, Molly's humour and fire,
toddler Harold sensing that incoming storm,
child Harold's fearful shock in
Barnardo's admitting studio.

And more:
>Ancestral English habitats:
>Impoverished, dense back alleys of Norwich;
>And hand-drawn mementoes reawakening
>gloriously narrow Yarmouth lanes.
>
>Grimsby East Pier, the Auction Room,
>Henry Mays, my great-great-grandfather,
>front and centre with his noble bow tie,
>showing off the catch landed
>from a herring drifter,
>light streaming from high windows
>back and right over a sea
>of northeast English peaked caps
>(and one rogue, perhaps a captain),
>merchants there to study the wares,
>some eyeing the camera, one sourly,
>two impassively, one impish grin between shoulders,
>Henry's eyes shining with pride and melancholy.
>
>Harold's abodes with Barnardo's:
>The glowering brick front of the
>Receiving House at Stepney Causeway, east London;
>The Clapham Home, styled as one of
>Dr. Barnardo's for Destitute Boys,
>a flag and pennant-bedecked line strung
>up high, while down below a little crowd
>awaits a Duchess;
>A cricket game on the road
>winding through the townhouses
>of the Boys Garden City;
>Two boys digging in a plot
>facing the tree-fronted
>seeming country house that was
>Teighmore on Jersey Island.

A windblown trio in 1929,
the Arthur brothers,
confident and strong,
flanking nineteen-year old Harold,
grown and still growing,
a glimmer of vulnerability
behind the slight smile.

Harold and Laura's wedding party,
tall broadly-smiling groom centre left,
Ken and Leita tucked firmly behind,
the place Harold's family might have been
occupied by the Wardell children and
the minister's family,
pensive bride and a
large bouquet centre right,
her sober family farther over.

A baby, my father, happily plopped
near a fence on Jackson's Farm;
And as a toddler working a pump handle;
And sitting in the cab of a gravel truck.

A smiling English trio in 1939,
a little day trip on a cool afternoon,
Molly and Albert leaning against a railing,
and, as always, Bertha, in her wheelchair,
blanket covering her lap and legs,
pretty dark cap perched at a stylish angle.

Harold's 1959 trip to England,
searching for roots and memories,
capturing his own images:
A seaside tourist pier near Grimsby
in the noonday sun;
And the port's busy harbour,

dawn gleaming white off a rowboat
and an ocean-bound trawler's bridge.

Harold laughing uproariously as he and two
buddies reel them in on a fishing trip;
Later cradling his first two grandchildren;
And then happily ensconced in his woodlot.

And still more: newly-found family,
myriad locales of the tale,
glimpses into so-called humble occupations,
departed and older generations young again.

Behold the dance, image and word,
partners seeking, needing each other
to complete the waltz through time.

14

Hope fulfilled: a baby boy, my father.
Hopes dashed: Laura's teaching career finished,
    frail fences, escaping cows—
And after two years the farm abandoned
and on to nearby Otterville and into a maelstrom of events:
    Driving gravel trucks part time for an Arthur brother;
    Then hired to drive full time for the town lumber yard;
    Come spring 1938, the yard's foreman and its driver, Ab and Harold,
    business acumen the first and daring personality the second,
    set up Byers & Wenn, their own business in neighbouring Norwich;
    Spooked by the War of the Worlds Hallowe'en broadcast
    Harold about to tear off for Manitoulin when the
    hoaxing truth revealed itself;
    And the birth of a daughter before the year was out.
Witness too the helping hands extended:
    Ab, husband of a school chum, offering a
    job, then friendship and partnership;

No credit available for Harold, but a loan obtained
through a neighbour;
A huge down payment to the young business
for a big job from his Grade 8 schoolteacher's husband;
A friend going to bat with town council
to get them a good deal on a business location.

Witness then, the transformation
from adversity to prosperity,
from hardship to accomplishment,
the business flourishing,
family completed with a second son.
And Harold reciprocated:
   Church Choir,
   School Board,
   Lions Club,
   Wartime Ontario Volunteer Constabulary.

Once a Home Child, an indentured,
downtrodden and beaten Barnardo Boy,
now successful, respected,
with family, friends and community,
looking back not in anger but forgiveness,
   Let bygones be bygones the motto,
   each Christmas easing away from hearth and home
   for an interval to visit Ken and Leita,
looking back not in anger, but with regret
   on a desert rather than a family tree,
looking back not in anger, but with
   nostalgic sadness on a
   childhood ripped away;
Looking forward to a 1959 return
   to England and a search for
   answers and reconnection.

An ocean away another saga

had been spinning out,
Henry, Eleanor, Freddy and
other souls long since passed on but
a living blood link still awaiting Harold:
Parents Molly and Albert,
and sisters Bertha and Kathy,
all in hometown Grimsby, and
half-brother Harry, less than
100 miles away in Leicester.
Albert, decades resigned from the
Merchant Marine, now
retired from a paper mill;
Kathy a married shop assistant;
Bertha the silent and still heart of the family;
Harry with his own family
having bounced through early jobs then
to the paper mill, then wartime parts for Lancasters,
finally surface-to-air missiles;
Molly, long-time caregiver to
Bertha and the others;

And a powerful, precious memory
of an empty cradle, a coerced signature,
assurance of care,
assumed decline and demise.

The 1959 Canadian visitor wings in and
finds childhood echoes and an
historic port in Grimsby,
finds sea breezes and orphanage
memories on Jersey,
finds Edie and other chosen family,
but finds the one elderly witness
to his long-ago adoption
stroke-bound and incommunicative;
And returns home with memories

but unfulfilled hopes,
with pictures and a trip journal
but unwritten family history,
without blood reconnection and
with a lifelong split unhealed,
assuaged by a childhood reclaimed,
the view henceforth forwards,
the past awaiting a future generation.

15
You should write this down.
My mother's words, a simple supplication
that pierced the dike of inertia,
allowed a river of pent-up tales to
burst forth and transform
modest tracts of curiosity
to flowering meadows of witness,
allowed torrents of voices to
course through in search of a humble outlet
to the sea of remembrance.

Writing, re-writing, expanding, revising,
mosaic pieced together pixel by pixel,
writing decade in and decade out;
Oft delayed, distracted by life's siren calls;
Oft delayed, waiting for release of illumination
as governments and institutions
slowly pulled back the shades;
Oft delayed but never abandoned;
Delineating family trees,
    locating in time and generation;
Diagramming maps,
    locating in space;
Swirling with the dance of visual and word.

Writing and searching,
a pursuit only understood
in looking back now,
internal drama then mirrored
in genealogical quest,
feeling for a stable platform
in emotional quicksand,
looking for the past to bolster my present,
longing for all those voices to fill a
lacuna deep inside, a hole where
my spirit should be—
and was, but walled-off and unseen,
Jennifer's long-interred feminine soul
shining through Jeff's
masculine cracks now and then,
his labour infused with
snatches of Jennifer's lyrical language,
flashes of her profound empathy,
a world, an era and a self
reimagined and restored,
Jeff's lifelong project, a testimonial torch passed
to Jennifer for completion and absolution.

16
Transformation.
Indentured child servant become
prosperous businessman;
Hardship and so many losses transformed
to humour and an eye for laughter;
Severed family ties turned into
the gift of grandchildren;
Maritime heritage and bloodlines
manifesting as a love
and mastery of fishing;
Urban and institutional beginnings

birthing a love of nature;
From a lifetime of work to
health-induced retirement in 1969.

More transitions overseas,
passings as the years flowed by:
father Albert, 1967;
sister Kathy, 1968, just 49;
adoptive sister Edie, 1971;
and, November's end 1973,
mother Molly, who had
tried to speak and unburden
but just could not, but who
never forgot her son Harold,
thought him long dead,
Molly never to know the truth.

Not a fortnight later,
a dozen days before Christmas,
that same son went for a winter walk to
find swans, feed ducks,
his heart taking the cue for its finale,
Harold to remain in the pond-side snow
until found by Ab, one last service
to his old friend and partner.

Grandpa's voyage here ended, and
my quest then began,
a search for answers,
a multi-faceted mission in
pursuit of identity rooted
in humanity, place and time,
the revealed trove exceeding
all imagination, triggering
pride in Grandpa's legacy,
pride in my family's legacy,

in the end discovering a drive
to leave my own bequest:
Blood links once broken by a
long-ago adoption and an
institutional fiat now forged anew,
Harry and Bertha uniting with me
and all of Harold's Canadian family to
reweave the tapestry of memory;
A virtual Dickensian pilgrimage from
an array of East Anglian villages,
venerable sea-obsessed Yarmouth and
the scabrous backstreets of Norwich
through Grimsby's mighty fishery and
then neo-Victorian orphanages to
southwestern Ontario agricultural servitude
and finally entrepreneurial triumph;
Version after version of my
testament quietly circulated
as the years rolled by,
as Harry, Bertha, Ab
and others left us;
Finally, the stories all told,
the images brought to life,
the vast ancestral chorus
and the choir of witness
singing out and shattering the silence,
Harold's chronicle fully unveiled,
and after forty years the
saga published in 2015.

Journey's close, seemingly.
But do they ever end? Maybe not.
The voices, the visions,
the footsteps are with me still,
the path forever unwinding
again and again somewhere

in memory's deep forest.
But the fruits are tangible,
the family bonds resurrected,
the river of oblivion forever bridged,
a proud history marching across.

Grandpa, I hope you like it.

Avian Odes

Great Horned Owl

Heard the commotion one sunny afternoon,
Saw you, huge and magnificent, alighting
High up in an oak. Persecuted by a
Coven of angry, fearful crows you
Retreated to Warbler Woods, and waited.
Called by preoccupations large and small
I never followed, until, years later,
Marcus' canine soul craved
Walks and woods hikes and
Pulled me out, into the green
Realm of trees and owls.
One evening, tarrying too long,
Dusk lay heavy, my sight failing but
Trust in Marcus' instincts held firm and
We forged on, racing dark, when came
Your haunting song floating through the leaves,
Heard for the first time but not the last,
> *Welcome to you who venture here,*
> *Welcome to my time,*
> *Welcome at last to my domain.*

Northern Cardinal

Amidst November's khaki mud
A crested carmine flash radiates life;
All through winter's alabaster somnolence
The steadfast crimson emblem radiates hope;
Resurrected vernal greens part for a
Black-masked scarlet epiphany;
And always nearby, his mate,
Gentle sandy olive streaked with glowing
Vermilion embers, now receiving the gift
Of a scrumptious seed,
Now just over in the cedar hedge,
A feeding duet as dawn steals in
And as dusk drops its veil,
The alpha and omega of my yard.
Summer nesting's love and protection
Flowers into hungry broods taken
To the feeders, traditions passed on;
Autumnal fires herald a turn of the wheel,
Crimson and tawn once more
To glisten through Nature's repose,
Forever connected,
Forever faithful.

House Sparrow

Overlooked as ordinary, drab, small,
The planet's most widely distributed avian,
Hanging around humans in
Gregarious flocks (safety in numbers).
Tackling my feeders in relays,
Socially singing in nearby bushes
And the deciduous hedge,
Always there, ubiquitous substrate
Of the wingéd world, spiritual cousins
Of the labourers and fishermen,
Crafts workers and servants,
Middle class and slum-dwellers
In my own family tree,
Pervasive ostinato over which
Flashier performers strut,
Seeming mundanity veiling
Unheralded nobility.

American Robin

Treasured spring portent, with your
Sunrise-emblazoned breast,
Nesting above the security light,
Sky blue eggs bursting into
Hungry mouths,
I envy you.

I envy your joy in everything:
Dash pause dash about the yard,
Listening for juicy worms,
Yanking out victims
To fill those eager little beaks;
Labours done, summer afternoons
Splashing happily in the bird bath;
Cheerily cheer up cheer up cheerily cheer up
Caroling dusk and early morning,
Chanting for life-giving rain,
Cheerily cheer up cheer up cheerily cheer up
You urge.

Sing it to me again,
Sing it to me tomorrow.

Mallard Family

While happily writing
On the Gaia House patio,
A relaxed recovery in New Hope,
I noticed the pair of you eyeing me,
Speculatively waddling past,
Gently throating to each other in Mallard.
Seemingly satisfied with the intruding guest
You issued beckoning quacks
But the three adolescents hanging back
Plaintively yawped teenaged refusals.
Beaking avian sighs, Mom and Dad,
You toddled a retreat and led the
Crew the long way around.

Canada Goose

The chill, glassy mist just then
Dissolving into hints of sultriness
Echoed with jubilant honks,
Avian position-signalling on high,
Pulling my gaze up to your magnificent
Flying V's northward bound
Flinging joyful vernal greetings.

Come the ordained crisp autumn day
The calls echoed again off frosted fields
As your arrow formations streamed south,
Bidding farewell until spring warmth
Once more crept in.

Winter past was deep, consistent;
Now it staggers all around,
Reeling under humanity's blows,
Glistening white morphs
To sulky brown mud,
Defiantly open water
Supplants sparkling ice.
Eminently flexible,
A few goose homebodies
Spawned many more of you that
Seize what's on offer, spurn the effort
And trade glorious flight for ungainly
Waddling about and strolls through traffic,
Expropriating luscious, manicured turf,
Cheerfully crapping all over your squattage;
Soaring nobility mutated to a
Grey-brown-black wingéd pest
Herded off the cathedral greensward
By a bellowing leaf blower;

Target practice for a skulking
Archer in a London park;
Clubbing victim of a sportsman
Whose putt was ruined by an
Inopportune anserine klaxon.

Undaunted, you multiply and toddle on,
Once a belovéd seasonal herald,
Now flocks of Cassandras trumpeting
Warnings, flaunting consequences,
Announcing a battle joined.

Mourning Dove

Blue jays and such blast in to the feeder,
Scattering skittish customers,
But not you.   Raptors circle,
Sending others for cover, but not you.
An objectively stupid bird,
Some will say, *zero survival instincts,*
Prolific breeders, but not much more.
I prefer unperturbable, untroubled,
Placid, peaceful, fatalistic.
Colours rather bland they sniff,
But look closer at the subtle palette
Of greys and beiges, with a whisper of
Pink. And no one can deny your
Mastery of sound, the thrum in flight,
And above all the plaintive call,
Spring and summer, soliciting a mate.
A joyous time one might think,
But the unforgettable, pleading tones
Seemingly infused with fathomless melancholy.
Maybe a way of evoking empathy,
Maybe a moan of dejection at being still alone,
Maybe a deep sadness in recognition of
Time passing, but the pensive heart
Resonates with profound sympathy.

Baltimore Oriole

Glorious hue of sunrise exploding into day,
Sunset's flaming herald of night,
Tiger lilies dancing in the sun,
Succulent fruit and a warming fire
On a chill winter evening,
My favourite colour and your hallmark,
Exerting a preternatural appeal,
The female's gentle warmth and
The male's blazing heat mated to jet black,
Your image now emblazoned on
A cherished tea mug, a memento of
Summer for long snowy days.

An elusive desideratum,
Three years in the wooing,
But once won, forever faithful,
Always returning early May,
Famished after the long migration and
In preparation for imminent nesting,
Gobbling down special jelly and
Slurping up delicious sugar water,
Enlivening the oaks with brilliant flashes
And fluting melodies or excited chattering.

Welcome home.

Black-capped Chickadee

Maybe it's the plaintive *feebee*
Early in mating season;
Perhaps the feisty *chickadee-dee-dee*
Warning of an intruder; or
Possibly the little black-crowned gray-buff
Figure darting in to snag a choice seed
From the feeder and dashing out to tuck it
Away in a bark crevice.
The manifestation may vary, but
You are there, somewhere,
Ever alert, first to find new food,
Hatching schemes to outwit and outlast.

Overtopped by soaring predators you
Zip in and out, never exposed for long;
Encircled by scavengers and competition
You outthink them all, eat what's on offer,
Spread the hoard in a multitude of
Never-forgotten nooks.
Endlessly adaptable, your eye is
Always on the main chance.

St. Lucian Parrot

Island rainforest hike in eighty-eight,
Marshall leading past scenic views,
Past an Arcadia perverted to charcoal pits,
And into the salvaged remains,
Greeting orchids and banana pods,
Meeting a local heading for a
Backcountry cockfight,
Cradling his wingéd warrior,
Wielding his prod stick. Skirting
Frankincense, orange, tangerine,
And, deemed worthy, we detour,
Down, across a stream, and up,
Dodging roots and vines, deeper,
Almost to the huge fig, and
Finally below the dead giant
Cradling new life above, to wait.
And wait.
And there, in the distance, parents,
Circling, landing, stealing in by indirection,
Warily scanning for predators.
We watch, silent, till
A riot of colour swoops in,
Green back and wings,
Dark blue and yellow tail,
Maroon-mottled breast,
Blue face, red neck,
Defiant survivors in a
Tiny hard-won enclave,
Still insisting on their place.
Time flowing on, ushered away
From the little family by
Sensitive mimosa, cocoa pods,
Cinnamon trees, a St. Lucian oriole,

Past grandmother's summer cottage
And the cockfight in full squawk,
Our spirits still back in the deep forest
Where Marshall's pride and joy
Nurtures and rebuilds.

My Grackle

Noisy and messy the received wisdom,
Labelled "Common", deemed
Tuneless and devoid of allure.
But as your flock outmuscles
Flashier and more melodious competition
Behold beauty in the charcoal body
And lustrous midnight-blue head,
Harken to the spiky language.
But in this ebony, clamouring mob
You were an anachronism,
An individual in a crowd
With your own mark of Cain,
A long white feather bifurcating your tail.
A mutant some would cry
With overtones of sci-fi disdain,
An abnormality, contrary to
Nature's Grand Design.
To me, something else: an artistic variant
Painted with a different brush,
A kindred spirit on the margins
Fighting to fit in, claim your place.
Each thaw I looked for you,
Proudly recording for FeederWatch your
Distinguished difference,
Until came that inevitable spring,
The returning host now
Monotonously uniform,
No flash of enlivening divergence;
But the collective soul remembers
And I will watch and wait;
May the kinship manifest again.

Auschwitz Threnody

*A belated response to experiencing the
Auschwitz-Birkenau Memorial and Museum.*

*For all of the victims and survivors whose suffering and
courage transcends all understanding.*

Inception

Ghastly residue of incomprehensible evil,
a realm of petrified torment and death and sublime heroism
and ghosts in staggering numbers;
every square inch, every stone,
the air itself, a holy cemetery;
a shrine of hallowed memory.
I was there in 2005, but different then,
Jeff still to the fore, Jennifer still waiting,
untransitioned,
my poetic feminine core shackled
deep within masculine armour.
So I was there, but with Jeff still my avatar,
part of a tourist family shuttled around with
a little clutch of strangers momentarily
united in slack-jawed shock,
united in variegated remembrance.
I saw, I heard, yet couldn't process, not really,
not then, not even for long afterwards.

But part of me remained within the wire,
incubating memories, listening to silenced cries,
gnawed by burgeoning awareness and an amorphous guilt,
wondering what spectres others came away with,
hoping we reverenced it all but afraid some
desecration crept in.

Lament by lament a hubristic, unnerving resolution took root,

given sustenance by a seismic collision,
Elie Wiesel's impassioned plea "We must remember!"
clashing with fearsome reborn echoes of the jackboots.
The call: to share what belatedly I so deeply felt,
to give voice to what my soul still seemed to hear,
to breathe a little humanity and individuality
into the vast valley of statistical bones,
a tiny repayment towards an eternal, ethereal debt.

How does one do this?
Weep in despair? Howl with rage?
Gasp in horror? Reel with nausea?
Cheer from the rooftops for transcendent
bravery and endurance?
Mourn the stunning physical and psychic deaths?
All that, and more, the hope, the need.

Now transformed to Jennifer
(who can attempt the voyage),
but awash in trepidation,
I set out onto this monstrous ocean,
latching onto specifics like a
shipwrecked woman clutching for a plank;
thus held afloat, we are borne along
by an irresistible, sacred riptide.

Invocation

Let me remember
(although,
how could I forget?)
Let who I have become
travel back there,
let the memories be
renewed and revealed,
let the clamouring multitudes
sing out and my voice
channel even a whisper.

Let me remember.
Let this soul see through
younger eyes,
let this spirit inhabit
my former form,
let the clamouring multitudes
sing out and my voice
channel even a whisper.

Starting from Kraków

Starting from Kraków,
mature, Canadian, Gentile,
born end of the fifties,
called by simple humanity to
make a family pilgrimage,
pay respects, to experience
the witness.
Called to build on pre-teen memories of
Dachau
        thunderbolt out of the darkness,
        locals shying away from giving directions.
Called to build on later memories of
Yad Vashem
        Israel's monument and memorial,
        names retrieved from oblivion,
        unfathomable horrors laid out,
        the Righteous Among the Nations
        given their place;
        the Hall of Remembrance,
        flickers from the eternal flame
        bouncing off abhorrent labels seared
        into history's soul,
        Dachau, Auschwitz, and more,
        sunlight bleeding through
        a high-up crack.
Called to go deeper, to
closer approach evil's heart.

Starting from Kraków,
begun on a hill surmounting
fire-breathing Smok Wawelski's
rumoured draconic abode,
a city by the 900's

bordering then bestriding
the Vistula.
Stare Miasto, the Old Town
          somehow spared
          World War II's agonies,
from St. Florian's Gate in the north
          last holdout of the medieval city wall,
          now a venue for artists' stalls,
past the red-brick rectangular
Gothic glories of St. Mary's Basilica
          home of the magnificent
          Viet Stoss altarpiece,
through the Grand Square
          largest in old Europe,
          domain now of buskers and mimes,
          vendors and pigeons,
and up Wawel Hill,
          realm of the Cathedral, a glorious agglomeration
          cradling dead Kings and Zygmunt's Bell
          whose immense tone requires twelve ringers
          (saved for special occasions, such as
          summer 1940's celebration of France's fall;
          Nazi overlord Hans Frank saw to that),
          and the great Castle
          standing guard over the river,
          an incredible congregation of
          Medieval Renaissance Baroque architecture.
Turn southeast, glance over Kaziemierz,
once Kraków's Jewish heartland,
home to teacher and philosopher
Benzion Rappaport, who pitched
his life's work out a
death-train window
          (miraculously found
          and later published),
lift the gaze farther,

a kilometre and a bit more,
over the bending Vistula and
hovering in the haze
will be a ghost quarter
haunting modernity,
traces still there of past agonies,
wartime Jewish ghetto,
mothers, fathers, families
once walled in and marked for slaughter.

Starting from Kraków,
leave Wawel and Stare Miasto behind,
head for a dragon's true home,
sixty kilometres west through
verdant peaceful countryside
          (wheeled human-stuffed abattoirs once
          rolled hell-bound just over there,
          the clanks and wails and groans
          echo yet through the fields and forests)
under dark, churning billows
glowering from above in
mortal combat with the sun and
into the waiting grasp,
just past the modest town of
Oświęcim.

Liberation

Auschwitz: the invader's name,
branded forever more in
humanity's consciousness.
Subdued clusters of pilgrims
ease from Parking Lot to Visitor's Centre,
where we find familiar enough ground.
Tour arrangements are made,
with a short Soviet Army film to start,
a victor's record for posterity,
scenes from camp liberation,
black and white, overlaid narration.

Many frames have faded
from my memory's view,
but some are granite-etched:
Bodies. Corpses.
Cadavers strewn like
dead leaves on snow
men women children
here piled like cordwood
there heaped like compost
dignity and dreams
annihilated
gentry working-class nobility
chucked together
agony-warped faces
gaping in frozen screams
long-scattered on icy wind
nausea even now lurking
just below my surface
despite heavy filtering
interposed.
What were the ghastly colours

burning the retina?
What was the putrid stench
oozing into every pore?
And look, staggering husks,
some of the long-term guests
now shrink-wrapped
suppurating skeletons
but the flame of life
not yet extinguished,
defying their torturers
with stubborn existence.

Enmeshed in putrefying
death and despair
how could one film, or help?
Beyond my powers, I fear.
How could one survive it?
Far beyond my limits.

Arbeit Macht Frei

Ahead, just past a gate,
former Polish Army barracks
subverted to a darker purpose,
deadly prison and headquarters,
now a haunted museum.
And above us,
prisonerslave Jan Liwacz's
dictated artifact still
leers down the
infamous Nazi greeting in
low-carbon rimmed steel
painted death-black
twisted into a gentle
lettered arch,
an old phrase
maladapted:
Arbeit Macht Frei
Work Makes You Free
or perhaps Work Sets You Free.
In this place,
free from what?
Free from life?
                happiness?
Not free from fear.
Certainly free from sincerity,
except genuine hatred
and suffering.
Work Makes You Free,
empty of truth but
oozing the dark energy
of a hideous joke;
Arbeit Macht Frei,
horror or humour,

the beholder shapes
the impact.
The words of the prisonerslaves
and the legions of the doomed
were devoid of impact
on the murderers
and torturers,
but not on history
or spirit.
Change context
change listener
and pivot
to eloquent
and moving
and heartbreaking
and potent;
words have
immense power,
power beyond imagining,
power of life and death,
of finality,
of miscreation.
Words spawned this,
words suckled it,
words of barbaric exclusion,
words of loathing,
words of evil,
ancient antisemitic hatred
        bloated,
        metastasized,
        modernized,
a black hole
devouring anyone
deemed different,
rallying cry for the
        bigoted

      ignorant
      racist
      sadistic
      cowardly
      desperate
      apathetic
      blind,
a lever to tyranny,
simple syllables
scuttling across the page,
cavorting in front of Klieg lights,
swaggering off on the fiery breeze,
goose-stepping forth
unbound,
mutated, inbreeding,
birthing demonic intention
contorted to action,
simple at first,
change some laws,
break some windows,
step by step,
round them up,
shoot them down
or pen them in,
one camp, then more,
step by step
until human and cultural
enslavement and
extermination
are bandied about
over stolen Cognac,
Wannsee's
ghastly inevitability,
a Final "Solution"
to the chain of
satanic "reasoning,"

all whelped from words
infused with the spirit of
Arbeit Macht Frei.
But look again.
Look closer at ARBEIT:
Here the B is upside down,
larger bulge precariously
balanced on top
in protest,
Jan's freshet of truth
in a vast swamp of lies
hiding in plain sight,
a seed of defiance
hopefully sprouting
in the sprawling jungle
of mockery
and brutality
and death.

Special Treatment

Our party prompted onward and impelled inward:
Block 11. Punishment block.
People as playthings for ostensible humans,
a variety of activities on tap:
>Sealed in like Poe's Fortunato,
>no light, near or actual suffocation;
>standing cell, four jammed in vertically
>every night, then out to slave labour;
>hands tied behind the back then
>hung by them from a beam;
>starvation; whipping; water torture;
>needles jammed under finger nails;
>branded with a red-hot iron;
>creative mutilation;
>imagination the only limit.

I peer into a dank cell, and am startled by
religious wall art, meticulously
inscribed with a fingernail
in the face of torment or worse,
>perhaps then taken to this nearby alcove,
>stripped naked and marched
>to the adjoining courtyard
(seen through a window),
>there to be chopped up with an axe,
>or doused in gasoline and set ablaze,
>or, for the privileged, up against
>a special pockmarked wall at one end,
>last support for those accorded
>the honour of a valuable bullet
>to the head or heart.

Glance down, eye tugged by

brave, grieving incongruity,
a phalanx of colour,
flowers and candles
radiating memory and loss.

Lift the gaze to the blacked-out
windows of the far wall:
Block 10. "Medical" experimentation.
Young women and girls as
lab rats for white-shrouded ghouls
inverting the Hippocratic Oath,
sterilization the obsession,
eliminate enslaved reproduction,
lay waste to the fount of life,
speed and efficiency the yardstick.
       Roll the dice: fry the pelvis with x-rays,
       wait, then a swift spinal and
       extraction of the ovaries for study
       from the restrained, terrified,
       watching guinea pig.
       Another toss: hideous injection,
       quick effect, screaming searing pain that
       reverberated through the whole block and
even now soars over the death wall
and across the decades,
ghostly shrieks melding into the
embrace of faith's hope and memory
painfully carved into a dank cell.

Reduction

Group by group we are ushered
to a series of tragic tableaux
of systematic pillage and degradation,
people priced and parcelled out
into piles of loot carefully
preserved in discrete bins,
each onion-life peeled
layer by layer.

Hair brushes.
       Your possessions are now theirs.
       No place here for beauty
       or pride in appearance.

Glasses.
       To the home front with them.
       Clear sight (physical anyway)
       a thing of the past.

Shoes (they'll take those) and
prosthetic limbs and crutches
(destined for wounded Nazi soldiers).
       Stumble or drag yourself forward.

Cups and bowls.
       They can use those too.
       No more eating or drinking
       with poise. Not that you will be
       doing much of that.

Baby clothes.
       Innocence untrammelled
       (until the very end),

lives unlived,
lambs to the slaughter
destined to be
soot and marsh infill,
their humble outfits deemed
to have more value;

bereft families swap
decent covering,
love and individuality
for striped, grieving rags
and numbered tattoos.

Hair.
Trying to shear away the
last remnants of dignity,
first step in bodily destruction,
sacred human remains recycled
into mattress stuffing and
socks for U-Boat crews.

Talleisim: Jewish prayer shawls.
Simple-seeming artifacts,
for their bearers imbued
with incalculable value,
now become prized
targets of desecrating repurpose,
one more stratum plundered,
articles of devotion stripped away;
faith seemingly naked and alone
like Job's on his ash heap
awaiting the whirlwind.

Petr's Suitcase

Confronted with the luggage bin,
each relic carefully labelled,
destruction's data points.
From the reverently
jumbled multitude
of ransacked wishes and lives,
nestled near Marie and Irene,
Herman and Klara,
one battered and broken
dreamcase pulled me in:
Petr Eisler, born March 20, 1942,
superfluously labelled Kinder, Child;
transported here,
I was told, May 1944;
final palindromic identity 6446,
daubed on twice for emphasis.
Staring in 2005 at your fractured holdall,
and remembering it now,
a cloud of questions swirls,
plaintive and insistent.

Who were you?
Born in the midst of war,
hope and life breaking through
death and despair,
a family favourite one would think,
possibly with one special toy.
Perhaps you walked and talked early;
or maybe took toddler-hood
at a leisurely pace.
The pain of second molars and
night terrors assuaged by
Mama and Papa's gentle ministrations.

No doubt you learned "No"
and, most especially, "Why?",
a child of violence and deprivation,
turning an ingenuous, immaculate
gaze on the world's madness and agony
even as its deadly currents
flung you here.

The train ride I can't imagine,
sardined into a near-airless tin
infused with vomit, urine and feces,
bodies dropping like autumn leaves,
starving, desperate for water,
eventually disgorged onto
that haunted platform.

The vision pulls me deeper,
and those questions keep
flooding over me:
Were the bustling, zebraed
enslaved scarecrows reassuring?
Did you have a teddy bear
quickly plucked from your grasp?
How you must have wondered
and quailed in the shadow of the
looming demonic uniforms.
Did you wail, causing one to
pick you up and silence your cries
with a whirl against an immutable boxcar?
Or were you as soundless as a tomb?
Were you separated from Papa
who was swept away shouting
your name?
Did Mama tell you this
was all a new game?
Did the billowing shower

speedily put you to sleep?
Perhaps, horrific thought, they ran low
on insecticide and pitched you
screaming straight into the flames.
Or maybe you choked and
fought to the last, trying
in vain to wake up Mama.

Forever just two years old,
what might you have become?
This world will never know,
but you entrusted us with
your fleeting journey that
flickers through a burst suitcase
and quietly beseeches
those passing by.

Rest in peace, Petr.

Faces and Fates

Pictures on a wall,
faces and fates of an
infinitesimal fraction,
frozen flashes of
shock, confusion, resignation,
emptiness, burning anger;
death sentences
delayed, for a bit,
in lieu of
toiling thralldom.

Scanning the array,
witnessing lives stripped down
to a few words,
what happened?
becomes my mantra
while I silently honour each
tragic, pleading image
as I search.

Stanislaw G, 30,
here nearly fifteen months;
victim maybe of one of the
legion of typhus-bearing lice,
time ended in fever and delirium.

Mieczyslaw I, 23 when you
arrived in January, 1941;
passing in April 1942, perhaps
by then a wasted, withered wraith.

Józef, 45, fifteen-month
term ended in June 1942;

I wonder if the finale was
shrouded in dysenteric
abdominal agony and diarrhea.

Zygmunt, 42; four months in
you may have looked
the wrong way at a guard and
been beaten to death
for such egregious
effrontery.

Mieczyslaw A, 30;
that fatal November day chills
my bones over time and distance;
it may have found you wracked with
painful coughing and gasping
for breath as pneumonia finished
you off.

Stanislaw Z, nearly 47;
after seven months here perhaps
you took matters into your
own hands and threw yourself
onto the electrified fence.

And on and on the anguished visions.
Into the youth room,
still searching.

Moses, 16, enslaved just a
month, early 1942.
A February-induced case of
frostbite leading to gangrene
spreading its deadly tentacles?

Kazimierz, just 14,

no death date, just
Did not survive.
Very early on you may
have collapsed at one
of the interminable
roll calls and quickly
been consigned to
the flames.

Anica, also just 14,
arrived July 1942,
Fate unknown.
What happened?
Maybe you made it
all the way to New Year's 1945,
only to crumple on an
aptly-named death march
out of here and been casually
chucked into a ditch.

And on and on,
students, artisans, farmers, academics,
each pair of haunted eyes proclaiming
I too had a story, worked hard, strove to find my place;
I too had a story, one replete with love and loss,
frustrations and triumphs large and small;
I too had a story, defied them while strength remained;
I too had a story of hopes and dreams.

But finally, there, just one,
high up in a corner,
Janina Bleiberg, 16,
unflinching gaze boring
through the photographer
to a point far beyond,
tagged Jude, Jew, surety here against

anything resembling decent treatment,
cast without Daniel into a lions' den
where women suffered more,
where some turned on their own
to escape the snapping jaws
a little longer.
Did you have some prized skill?
Maybe musical, for the camp orchestra
which serenaded starving work details;
or perhaps languages, so orders from
the overlords were unambiguous;
but maybe an extraordinary synthesis
of stamina, courage, wits and luck
stood alone.
Janina Bleiberg, 16, arrived May 30 1942,
well over two and a half years
chained up in the dragon's cave,
over thirty-two months lashed to
four rampaging Apocalyptic horsemen,
the culmination embodied on the label
in one blazing, triumphant word: *Survived*.

A chorus of silenced voices flows
from all the other frames,
We too had stories of
hopes and dreams and tragedy;
we too passed through here, but
were trampled by those lethal riders.
You who survived,
you who come after,
bear witness.

Cyclone

First experimental dungeon, seeking
efficient despatch of souls deemed surplus,
small, bare, clammy chamber featuring
only overhead primitive outlets waiting
to vaporize and spew deadly effluent.
A voice from a whirlwind no longer,
now Leviathan straining at its chains,
roaring forth a raging tempest imprisoned
in little blue pellets of repurposed pesticide,
frozen embryonic shards of terror and doom
labelled Zyklon, Cyclone.

Death seeps from every stone,
oozes up my leg, gasping ghosts
lurch and careen around and through me
in vain search of mortal raiment
long since tumbrelled over there
and pitched into oven-shaped
black holes and denatured into smoke and ash.

But venture even deeper, two more kilometres
towards the sun's barrow, near a little
village named for birch trees,
the German designation forever
scorched across time and memory: Birkenau.

Under the watch tower and
through the rust-brick death gate
where so many tramped to the gas chambers
before efficiency demanded a special track;
swallowed up in the stultifying vastness,
hike all the way to the back:
Leviathan fully unleashed,

belching miasma and flame,
thundering hatred and death.
Four immense engines of
extermination now in ruins,
one burned during an incredible
revolt, then dismantled,
>   *break the teeth in their mouths;*
>   *tear out the fangs*
the others, with Judgment closing in,
a desperate attempt to erase history,
camouflage abomination.
>   *I will speak in the anguish of my spirit;*
>   *I will complain in the bitterness of my soul*
Heaped wreckage lies in front of me,
but mind's eye is trained on the
museum's model, evil incarnate reconstituted.
>   *your life shall hang in doubt*
>   *before you, night and day you shall*
>   *be in dread*
Invisible sepulchres mount to the clouds
and beyond, like the death wall marked with
"a phalanx of colour,
flowers and candles
radiating memory and loss."
>   *destroying both young man and virgin,*
>   *the suckling child with the man of gray hairs*
A terrible journey took them here.
One last glance at radiant sun, or waltzing clouds, or
gleaming moon, or feathery, wafting snow,
one last draught of open air,
then down these now-ruined steps, just there.
>   *For the thing I fear comes upon me,*
>   *and what I dread befalls me*
Driven like vermin down the now
rubble-filled underground hall
to the first room,

stripped of clothes, stripped of dignity,
stripped naked in body and soul,
but clothed in glowing humanity.
>*Why dost thou stand afar off, O Lord?*
>*Why dost thou hide*
Then, a little farther down, crammed
into a lethal womb festooned with
ostensible shower heads,
>*I waited for light, darkness came*
awaiting the cyclone, waiting for Zyklon B to
sting the chest, seize the brain,
lock up red blood cells,
shut down the lungs.
>*I am dismayed, and shuddering seizes my flesh.*
>*Why do the wicked live…*
>*and grow mighty in power…*
>*They send forth their little ones like a flock,*
>*and their children dance…*
>*They spend their days in prosperity*
The sounds that ricocheted around these blocks and slabs:
the screech of the bolts slamming into place,
>*All this has come upon us,*
>*though we have not forgotten thee,*
>*or been false to thy covenant*
the gentle hiss of gas wafting in,
>*how long shall the wicked exult?*
>*They crush thy people*
the shrieks and groans and wails
>*I cry to thee and thou dost not answer me*
and prayers.
>*Have mercy on me…*
>*I hold fast my righteousness, and will not let it go*
And then, in that same space,
final moments,
some gently slipping away,
many in agony, clawing at the walls,

or their throats, or each other,
>   *the terrors of death have fallen upon me.*
>   *Fear and trembling come upon me,*
>   *and horror overwhelms me*
some, maybe, reaching through death's veil.
>   *with all my heart, and with all my soul,*
>   *and with all my might*

I try to turn away, but am
drawn irresistibly to imagining
the emotional torrent;
utter failure.
And yet spectres invade me and flow through:
Burning cheeks, flushed with anger at
human-shaped husks of hate allowed
free rein,
>   *The wicked draw the sword and bend their bows,*
>   *to bring down the poor and needy,*
>   *to slay those who walk uprightly;*
>   *their sword shall enter their own heart*
heat doused by ice slithering through my veins,
convulsing heart, mind, soul and body,
>   *why hast thou forsaken me?*
>   *Why art thou so far from helping me*
tumbling into a mournful bolero with empty darkness,
>   *behold, for I am despised.*
>   *Is it nothing to you, all you who pass by?*
>   *Look and see*
>   *if there is any sorrow like my sorrow*
slip from night's clasp, defiantly
reach for a latent dawn.
>   *Even though I walk through the*
>   *valley of the shadow of death,*
>   *I fear no evil;*
>   *For thou art with me...*
>   *Thou preparest a table before me*

in the presence of my enemies...
I shall dwell in the house of the Lord
for ever.

Release visions, step a little farther:
Under this pile of rubble the enslaved
Sonderkommandos, all male, swung into action.
Yank apart the Gordian Knot of contorted corpses
(perhaps finding your liquidated wife, or son, or daughter),
drag out the murdered by neck or feet, then process:
shave hair, rip out gold teeth, pry into
orifices for hidden wealth,
knowing your turn could be coming
at any time.
O that I had wings like a dove!
I would fly away and be at rest
Then load into blazing ovens,
that now-collapsed house of cards just here;
later remove ash and detritus,
grind stubborn bone fragments
with mortar and pestle, pile up
for recycling or, perhaps,
(in the guards' parlance)
fish food in the Sola River.

Behold the Genesis Flood reborn
in fume and flame, but
no ark here, no wingéd companions
to scout for fury's abatement.
Behold multi-faceted, unfathomable evil
triumphant
until the wheel turned again,
for in the space left by light's hibernation
darkness shaped as humanity
blitzkrieged through, each of the many
hundreds of thousands of victims,

no matter age, gifts or condition,
a child of God.

Look up. Into that same sky smoke billowed
twenty-four hours a day, taking with it
priceless memory, tradition, wisdom;
incalculable potential and energy, and babies unborn;
incalculable arts and sciences, a kaleidoscope of labour,
and on and on,
all incinerated to soot and ash,
each precious candle brutally
snuffed before its time
through fear and deadly indifference
by vampiric shades cringed at day's gestation
amidst legions of swirling, questioning spirits.

Dark Chronicle

The gallows are still here on which
he was hung close to the Commandant's villa,
dancing in the death-laden air
near where his children frolicked:
Rudolf Höss, overlord of annihilation.
Recoil is tempting, but the question
is all-pervading and insistent:
How?
How could one witness,
how could one execute,
how could one command
all this?
Men, women, children
deemed parasitic mortal enemies,
stripped of all they knew,
crying to God,
      to each other,
      to your underlings,
      to you,
marched day after day after day
into gas and flame,
a select few retained for
slavery and experiment,
death awaiting in ways
uncountable and unimaginable.
How?

A potential Rosetta Stone
reposes in a display case,
precise handwriting
marching across the page:
Höss' memoirs, written in the
shadow of the noose, later

published as a cautionary tale of sorts.
Spelunk into the chronicle, expecting a
suitably hideous henchman
for his monstrous bosses
Heydrich and Himmler,
some archetype from the hellish
Nazi menagerie of horror
       (a twisted psychopath,
       a brutal sadist,
       a seething cauldron of antisemitic hate)
and find something worse:
Not warped *Sturm und Drang*
but a matter-of-fact confession,
engaging, informative prose
modelling his adamantine psychic fortress
erected stone by stone with
tireless cranes forged from
blind adulation of strength allied
to post-Great War bitterness
hunting for a scapegoat,
coolly detached dehumanization
striated through the soil;
a mental citadel whose narrow
befouled windows
reduced the pleading masses to
empty shapes obscured by
slavish devotion to orders,
an infestation to be controlled
at all costs, the only concession
an extermination deemed more "humane",
dying cries penetrating his
hidden chambers and halls but
drowned out by booming echoes of
technical precision, efficiency, and deluded duty,
silenced by a glowering, toothbrush-mustached
altar bleeding the slogan

All who are not of good race in this world are chaff.

I cast about for a semblance of a soul,
and am assailed by echoes modulating to
tales of bureaucratic nightmares,
interpersonal rivalries and politics,
supply shortages, useless subordinates,
an earnest debate between Pohl's enslavement
and Eichmann's eradication
as the desperate wisps outside the walls
scream on their futile whispers.
Casting about, finally beckoned by a
drifting, ghostly memory that was
seduced by goose-stepping words,
disincarnated by tragic choice
and an SS uniform,
driven to dark corners by
cultish devotion to a ghastly mission.

But come down into the crypt
and find him as a boy who wanted
to be a priest, a boy broken
by an assumed betrayal
of his confessional,
light and life blindly forsworn
step by step,
divine faith perverted to fatal
mesmeric idolization of
Party and Power
vaulting upward
from these innocent depths
stone by stone
to the peaks of the deathly edifice
throwing fiery shade
on the ensouled multitudes
deemed chaff.

And at the very end?
Letters and a visiting priest
point to realization,
the choking anguish of the
leviathanic spectral cortège finally heard.

But this world cannot judge that,
this world immeasurably scarred
for eternity by his command.

Pink Triangle

A sneering macabre ostinato grounding
the entire horrisonant din,
Nazi mania for speciation of the condemned,
rooted in the infamous yellow star,
branding as accursed an
ancient faith, culture and tradition.
Here in Auschwitz the star modulates
to a clamorous fugue of triangles:
    Green for professional criminals;
    Black a grab bag labelled asocial, swallowing up
      the Roma, sex workers, the homeless, and more;
    Red for "political" prisoners;
    Purple signifying Jehovah's Witnesses;
    Yellow for the Jewish people, overlaid with another
      triangulated colour to achieve the mandated star.

But there, one more theme weaving in,
plaintive and forlorn—the pink triangle,
mocking label dominated by men condemned
only for loving other men;
but slipping into the silences,
also condemned for their inner flames,
my sisterhood, female spirits
tearing at contrary, shrouding male shells.
Blessed to be born in a different time and place,
now transitioned from Jeffrey to Jennifer,
my newly integrated mind's eye sees
chambered Jeff myopically scan the display case
and pass on (Jennifer from her subconscious prison
 insistently importuning but heard as
just a mysterious, fleeting susurration).

Miles and milestones later my memories

are remade, imbued with new meaning,
and pen in hand I spiral through that pink triangle,
tripping over the decades, to the '20's of
another century, an entr'acte between
violent cataclysms, and wondering,
what if this was my time,
what would I have been?
Most places a tormented butterfly locked
in imperishable masculine amber,
tagged pervert, insane, degenerate,
never to feel the sun or hear my wings
whisper on the wind;
but Weimar-period Germany,
the Great War then a nightmare past,
Hitler a distant rumble expected to fade;
daring, decadent, doomed Weimar,
its beating heart at blazing Berlin,
an ephemeral roiling crucible,
a time of Bauhaus, Albert Einstein and Thomas Mann,
Brecht and Weill's *Threepenny Opera*,
Marlene Dietrich and *The Blue Angel,*
prostitution, drugs and the black market,
wildly uninhibited cabarets,
and much, much more,
a tumultuous symphony spacious enough
for even my pioneering sisters to have a part,
tremulous but growing:
Permits to publicly present our true selves;
Magnus Hirschfeld's research and medical Institute;
our own magazines and nightclubs,
headlined by the infamous, amazing Eldorado;
above all being seen and heard,
casting off shame and having community.
Maybe there I could have shattered
the unyielding chrysalis and found my voice.

Then the clanging chimes at midnight
proclaimed onslaught of the Hakenkreuz
and its minions;
diversity now deemed noxious plague,
the entire pink cohort, gay and trans (in modern terms),
repudiated by families and former friends,
pilloried, hounded,
step by step,
books burned,
Hirschfeld's Institute torched,
Eldorado perverted to Nazi headquarters,
arrested,
peoples of all the triangles designated for
thralldom and disposal in the camps
where pink sank into the abyss:
Given the most arduous assignments,
despised even by other prisoners,
many driven to suicide,
their SS slavers incited to new depths of depravity
all because our inner stops
reverberated with chromatic notes;
and mine, no doubt, would have
been deftly snuffed, never to be re-sounded.

Witness a curtain crashing down,
our little song crushed by an
ushered-in Götterdämmerung
hemorrhaging death and hate,
a scene repeated over and over
like a record needle stuck on
Wagner's lyrical savagery.
My forgotten sisters and brothers,
revealed or hidden, self-aware or suppressed,
we have always been here;
but this time was different: you were
convention-shakers, mould-breakers, trailblazers,

and came the howling midnight klaxons
you paid audacity's highest price, and,
obliviated or not, were pitched with
so many others into hell's waiting maw.

Now here I am, comfortable (but for the
unceasing etheric chorale),
awed, guilt-stained, grateful, scribbling.
I shed lonely tears of pride, for
before those fatal klaxons
my sisterhood fought another war,
invisible, soul-deep,
one I know well,
a desperate sub rosa pas de deux,
shame and hope whirling on the razor's edge,
and all those decades ago hope
flung aside the inherited, imposed
manly shroud,
divine feminine spiritus
finally dancing free like
evanescent will-o'-the-wisps amidst a marsh.

Turning, I sing out that your lives had
value and meaning;
I quiver with anger at the assassins
who tormented and butchered you,
and others like us to this day;
horribound and uncomprehending
I weep for your suffering,
a profound drop in a bitter,
agonized ocean.
May these few words be a
memorial from one who, having seen it,
cannot and will not forget,
and who honours and exalts
the hidden realm of the pink triangle.

Vista

Tramp up the infamous Birkenau gatehouse
mounting the aperture through which
trains plunged to spew their wretched contents;
stunned as the enormity springs into view
stretching way off left, right and ahead,
(and this only one sector of the lair);
some buildings still stand vigil,
many now reduced to scars on the landscape;
the wrecked furnaces squat
ten minutes' pilgrimage straight on,
under a sky slipping to sickly gray.

The ghastly scene incarnates before me even now,
camera bag strap once more digging,
disbelief seeps back in,
what-ifs worm out from under
dislodged psychic rocks and weave
    time-spanning phantasmagorical webs
        that clutch and cling, remould and rescript:

          Adjust the strap and shift the rifle,
          most prominent accessory
          to the uniform, but the coup de grâce
          gleams on the collar:
          twin lightning bolts, imperishable
          symbol of drilled-in duty that
          displaced nearly all, service that
          includes standing up here, while days,
          images, sounds, smells kaleidoscope together.

          The cries float up here, fading
          in and out like mid-summer fireflies:

> *Mama!*
> > *Papa!*
> *Water!*
> > *Where are we?*
> > > *What is happening?*
> *Mamme!*
> > *Papa!*
> *Vaser!*
> > *Vi zenen mir?*
> > > *Vas tut zikh?*
> *Mama!*
> > *Papa!*
> *Viz!*
> > *Hol vagyunk?*
> > > *Mi történik?*
> *Mama!*
> > *Papa!*
> *Woda!*
> > *Gdzie jesteśmy?*
> > > *Co się dzieje?*

Weather gods play games sometimes;
today's result is a frozen blast
off the Carpathians

> *Mutti!*
> > *Vati!*
> *Wasser!*
> > *Wo sind wir?*
> > > *Was ist los?*

From malignant undertone a
faint pulsing hum slips in,
steady crescendo as steel wheels
hammer out a relentless beat;
baleful warning tones
swell to piercing shrieks,
distant smudge to choking fumes

as another shipment screeches
beneath and to terminus
     Maman!
          Papa!
   L'eau!
       Où sommes-nous?
          Qu'est-ce qui se passe?
Restless night pierced,
floodlights frame silhouettes,
some lost, some cajoling and
mouthing sweet nothings to the
Zyklon-bound procession
     Mamme!
          Papa!
   Vasser!
       Vi zenen mir?
         Was tut zikh?
     Mama!
          Papa!
   Water!
       Waar zijn we?
         Wat gebeurt er?
A flicking white glove
left, left, left, right, left
death, death, death, death later, death
     Mama!
         Očka!
   Voda!
       Kje smo?
         Kaj se dogaja?
Snaps and snarls, barbaric yawping
havoc straining to be let slip
     Mama!
         Tata!

Vada!
       Dzie my?
              Što adbyajecca?
Out beyond the white glove
the bakery roars on,
belching smoke and flame
and ashy flecks of the last shipment

     Mama!
         Papa!
Viz!
       Hol vagyunk?
           Mi történik?
     Mamá!
         Papá
Neró!
       Pou eímaste?
           Ti symvaínei?
Appelplatz—roll call: Jagged grids
shouted and clubbed into order,
stationary through an eternity as the
almighty count is done and redone.
Every so often a vertex drops;
more fuel for the bakery

     Mutti!
         Vati!
Wasser!
       Wo sind wir?
           Was ist los?
Petr! Petr! Mein Sohn! Meine Frau!
     Mama!
         Tata!
Voda!
       Gde smomi?
           Šta se dešava?
Strutting peacocks and peahens,

often jumped-up prisoners,
bellowing, brandishing, looking
for an excuse, any excuse

     Maman!
         Papa!
   L'eau!
        Où sommes-nous?
          Qu'est-ce qui se passe?
Crunchcrack..moan..
crunchcrack..moan..
repeat until silence.
No need to look—
an excuse was found

     Mama!
         Papa!
   Woda!
       Gdzie jesteśmy?
         Co się dzieje?
     Mama!
         Papa!
   Paji!
       Kaj sinem akate?
         Avilo kaj čimuni?
Red letter day today: Behold
the big wheel from Berlin
gaze on with smug, impassive
approval

     Máma!
         Tati!
   Voda!
       Kde jsme?
        Co se děje?
Bada dum Bada dum Bada dum dum dum
A work detail tramps out to the
strains of the Radetzky March,

courtesy of the Camp Orchestra,
slaves spared the gas (for now)

    Mama!
        Tata!
  Voda!
      Gdje se malazimo?
        Što se događa?
Blazing heat this afternoon, too much
for this uniform; no doubt more
vertexes will collapse at Appelplatz

    Mamme!
        Papa!
  Vaser!
      Vi zenen mir?
        Was tut zikh?
    Mamma!
        Papà!
  Acqua!
      Dove siamo?
        Che cosa sta succendendo?
Unbelievable and indescribable stench,
burning meat and hair drown you and invade
every pore, seasoned with a healthy dose
of the unwashed and rotting, plus a soupçon
of shit; it's everywhere down there

    Mamá!
        Papá
  Neró!
      Pou eímaste?
        Ti symvaínei?
The work detail trudges in,
cudgelled all the way, dragging
dead bodies

    Mama!

    Papa!
  Paji!
     Kaj sinem akate?
      Avilo kaj čimuni?
Percussive polkas, duets of
whipcrack and scream slash
hulking air
   Mama!
     Papa!
  Viz!
     Hol vagyunk?
      Mi történik?
   Mama!
     Papa!
  Water!
    Waar zijn we?
     Wat gebeurt er?
Finger the trigger,
gaze down,
nothing but shapes,
shapes staggering through
a vast graveyard
   Mama!
     Ocko!
  Voda!
    Kde sme?
     Čo sa deje?
   Mamá!
     Papá!
  Agua!
    Onde estan mis djenitores?
     No se ke pasa ayi.
There, just over the trees,
feeble flickers behind the
gloating smoke and ash,

sun once more losing the battle
Mama!
Papa!
Woda!
Gdzie jesteśmy?
Co się dzieje?
Searchlights gambol from the towers,
frolicking to the permeant buzz
of the electrified fence
Mama!
Papa!
Water!
Where are we?
What is happening?

Shocked into action, those collar-bound
gashes sizzle and spark,
explode and brand my marrow
as the mangled spider coiling on the flag
swells and bloats, engulfing me in a
searing, sightless miasma;
swept and spun down past
upward-soaring numinous flights,
down and stripped of all but memory,
through that now-breaking
sickly gray sky

to the Cyclops straddling a train breach
where multilingual murmurs caress the air,
and bedecked once more in tourist attire.
Below, puddles from a fleeing cloudburst
flank the paths graced by other
voyagers, all on journeys of
mourning, remembrance and discovery,
each carried by choruses of

prayers and questions,
one lady quite still, staring over
the deathly vastness.

Swathed in the luxury of
a different time and place,
and in reflecting back,
Hadean webs fiss and fade,
what-ifs slither off, for now,
but a scar remains,
shape indeterminate,
but soul deep.

Leib and Maximilian

1 the good shepherd...
Another tour memory,
ushered to one more cell,
final home for those starved
in collective retaliation
for an escape or the like;
one small window leaks light,
artifacts materialize through bars:
Three large candles, one reaching higher
than a ghostly kneeling supplicant;
and a sign, venerating one victim:
Father Maximilian Kolbe.

Born in Poland 1894,
German father, Polish mother,
gifted a vision of the Virgin Mary at 12,
and soon at an ethereal divergence
contemplating holy orders
beside Rudolf, a boy who would be
the Auschwitz Commandant:
This other strode down
an ever-darkening path,
Maximilian to the priesthood.

Franciscan friar,
teacher in Kraków,
founder of a monastery,
missionary in Asia,
back to Poland 1936.
Hold fast through the Nazi hurricane,
refuse cover of German paternity,
hide refugees, including Jews,
step by step,

issue anti-Nazi publications,
arrested February 17, 1941,
Auschwitz May 28.

Insistence on priestly vocation
led to crunchcrack and whipcrack;
come high summer one of those escapes
meant ten prisonerslaves,
none Maximilian,
packed off to the starvation dungeon,
Franciszek Gajowniczek crying
       My wife! My children!
Maximilian interceded;
a few words, a quiet gesture, but
a monumental moment amidst an
eon of despair and horror:
He took Franciszek's place,
led others in prayer as they
shrivelled and faded
one by one,
until after two weeks he was alone
in death's antechamber.
Nazi patience exhausted, he was killed
with an injection of carbolic acid.

And Franciszek?
Survived to bear witness,
attend Maximilian's canonization,
and contemplate this cell, whose
pitiless portal he never crossed.

2 *I call to remembrance my song in the night...*
At the end of the track:
Fields of slaughter,

punctuated by the shattered crags
of Crematoria II and III;
Fields of enthralment
for the Sonderkommandos
who pulled out the slain, "processed",
and loaded insatiable furnaces;
Fields of teeth, buried by those same slaves,
who expressly have
strewn them all over the terrain,
as many as we could, so that the world
should find material traces of the millions
of murdered people;
Fields of memory, forever expiring
history, suffering, butchery, defiance;
reliquary for inestimable memoirs,
including Salmen Gradowski, who wrote of teeth;
and Leib Langfus, rabbi and rabbinical judge
of Maków, Poland.

Leib was seized, shipped to the
Mlawa ghetto November 1942,
then Auschwitz December 7,
wife and son annihilated immediately,
Leib consigned to the Sonderkommandos;
holding to his truth and refusing some duties,
incredibly reassigned to
sweeping the Crematoria courtyard
and preparation of gassed women's hair
for those Nazi mattresses and socks
as the ovens blazed on.
But burning brighter still, determination
to lacerate the necrotic pall:
Pray over the assassinated;
Steal priceless minutes from death's jaws
to somehow record, commemorate,
celebrate and condemn,

plant hopeful seeds of witness,
one day, miraculously,
to see the light, including
>600 screaming, pleading, crying children
>jammed into a gas chamber, smiles creeping
>onto SS faces only after pesticide-induced silence.
>>*Have they never had any children?*

>Passover 1944, Boyaner Rebbe Moshe Friedman
>excoriates a Nazi officer, telling him
>they would pay tenfold for
>each murdered Jewish soul,
>leads his whole group in the
>Sh'ma Yisra'el prayer,
>then marches off to his doom.
>>*This spiritually exalted moment, without*
>>*a precedent in human life...*

>A mixed cohort of Jews and Polish Catholics
>being driven to massacre, a Polish girl
>asks the Sonderkommandos to tell her people
>that she and her comrades died as heroes,
>the whole group rising in song,
>the Poles their national anthem,
>the Jews the Hatikva, future anthem of Israel.
>>*A terrible and cruel fate has ordained*
>>*that the lyrical sounds of these different*
>>*anthems mingle in this accursed corner*
>>*of the globe.*

Leib turned to more drastic action,
helped plan a desperate revolt to
blow up an engine of extermination.
October 7, 1944: plot discovered,
insurrection flares, escapes made,
three SS killed;

revolt crushed, escapees
and many more murdered but
Crematorium IV torched and crippled,
over there in the corner,
a breathtaking spoke in the
wheel of destruction.

Last diary entry:
> *Now we are being taken into the*
> *zone. The last 170 remaining of us.*
> *We are certain we are going to meet*
> *our death. 30 people have been*
> *selected to stay in Crematorium number V.*
> *Today is November 26, 1944.*

Eye-witnessed culmination:
Urgently bury the priceless testimony;
step out of the execution line,
confront SS officers;
final words to his soot-bound contingent:
> *...let us now go to meet death bravely and with dignity!*

3 *...they shall mount up with wings as eagles*
Job on his ash heap won a victory:
Demanded a response from the whirlwind
and was answered, albeit
with question after question
> *...who shut in the sea with doors...*
> *and said "Thus far shall you come,*
> *and no farther..."*

Maximilian and Leib, two
who took up that challenge,
redirected it to evil on earth:

Thus far...
      Bodies forfeited to
      ravage and ruin
...and no farther
      Heart, mind, will and,
      for them, faith impregnable.
And legions more who also
heard that call, each answering
in their own way.

Now pause, be still,
touch the teeming air,
listen to the murmuring walls,
that spirit is still here;
it gleams in the corners of
this oubliette become memorial,
softly soars over the
blasted wracks and the
meadows of volcanic memory,
slips inside us through a crack
to whisper and echo.

Memorial Plaque in 23 Languages

For ever let this place be
a cry of despair
and a warning to humanity,
where the Nazis murdered
about one and a half
million
men, women and children,
mainly Jews
from various countries
of Europe

Auschwitz-Birkenau
1940-1945

Consider a Million

Consider a million.
Just the first million.

Mourn a million sagas brought
to a choking halt right here,
in this infernal spot.

Feel a million silenced souls
watching you.

Queue their corpses head to foot
from that odious gatehouse all the way to
Crematoria II and III at the back;
keep going, give everyone their space,
and so repeat, over and over,
1,840 times to accommodate them all.

Carefully bestow each of the murdered
into a casket, form one precarious tower
that soars more than a hundred miles
past the International Space Station.

Line up a million vigilants,
one for every shattered life,
shoulder to shoulder along
the highway westbound from
Auschwitz; watch that line
snake on and on and on
to Berlin and 30 miles past.

Listen while each vigilant
says the name of their martyr,
one after the other, day and night;

and still find yourself listening
34 days later.

Devote twelve hours a day
to reading obituaries, just
five minutes apiece;
fold the last newspaper
nineteen years from now.

Scan the memorial book, only
one line for each of the million;
all 16,667 pages of it.

Hallow a million funerals,
one by one round the clock,
every one a short hour
to pray, to eulogize,
to say goodbye and to grieve,
to remember and honour
the lost but not forgotten;
the final amen 114 years in the future.

Feel a million silenced souls
seize your spirit and voice,
striving always to cry and sing out.

Behold a million candles,
their humble flickers melded into one,
a glorious wafery spire of radiance
streaming heavenward through the night
more than a hundred feet high.

Stretch out, they're all around;
consider each extraordinary
one of that million;
and so many more.

Envoi

Brick, wood, stone, wire, grass;
whole, wrecked, restored, burnt;
petrified cairns of an inconceivable
conquering nightmare that
drove the shattered remnants
of normality into the realm of
nebulous dreams; a shrine of
mute, eloquent witnesses always
waiting to testify, watching me
bid a hushed farewell as
I retreated through
peaceful, verdant countryside
that still murmurs echoes of hell-bound
human-stuffed cattle cars,
to venerable Kraków,
and then home, part of me
forever left behind within the razor wire
and suitcase packed with ghosts but

engulfed in a stupefying cloud,
eyes yet to see,
ears yet to hear,
spirit yet to feel,
but in time the shadows
slipped in and around,
whispering, persistent,
swelling to a haunting, ethereal chorale,
and, finally, soul to paper
attempted,

delving into remembrance,
a meagre, belated witness to shards
of the incomprehensible,

adamantine psychic fortresses of inhumanity
that glower from every brick and blade of grass,
fear beyond conception bleeding from
every torture cell and death chamber,
bravery and endurance and despair
far outside my ken that stares back
from picture frames and display cases,
the air thick and resonant with
a hymn of beautiful and tormented melodies
slashed through by screeching chords
that crash into wire and tracks
and set them shuddering with
"Why?" and "How?" and "What if?"
and splinter the sky
with coloured triangles
branding the prey,
green, black, red and purple,
endless arrays of yellow for the Jews,
and my little pink cohort,
condemned for their chromatic notes
which join the surging, desperate chorus of
"Never Again!"

only to be met with screams of
panic and death from
Cambodia, Rwanda, and more,
entwining with that anguished symphony
which despite deadly horror and the struggle to survive
is infused with sacred strains of
kindness and hope and devotion,
some bolder like Rabbi Langfus'
resistance and testimony,
and Father Kolbe's sacrifice,
others, many, of subtler but deep tonality:
      Suppress your own tears and terror
      so you can comfort your child;

        quick advice to a new inmate
        fresh off the train,
        look strong, lie about your age;
        scrounge a good rag for a
        bunkmate's frozen feet;
        smuggle a precious piece of rotten potato
        or a crust of bread for someone
        even hungrier than you;
        carry a shovel for a weaker member
        of your work detail;
        loving words for one drowning in hate;
        tend to a fellow slave burning with fever;
        smuggle gunpowder under a ragged dress
        bit by bit to build a supply for a
        revolt against the Crematoria;
        ease the passing of a martyr breathing their last;
        for those who miraculously lived,
        the audacity of memory and testament,
        somehow try to portray the unimaginable,
        keep renewing that cry of "Never Again!",
        remember the silenced millions,
a mission accepted by Filip Müller
who testified to Leib Langfus' final moments;
Filip, who tried slipping into a gas chamber
with the doomed to end his pain,
only to meet one of unfathomable nobility,
a girl known now only to God,
who urged him back:
        We must die, but you still have a chance to save your life…
        You have to return to the camp and tell everyone about our last
        hours…
        …perhaps you'll survive this terrible tragedy and then
        you must tell everyone what happened to you

but I was not there, in
Elie Wiesel's *kingdom of night,* as he was,

I did not see, in his words,
> *the old men and women whispering the ancient prayers...*
> *the children, frightened and forlorn,*
> *all part of a nocturnal procession walking towards the flames,*
> *rising to the highest heavens*

I did not walk with those
whose bodies survived but whose spirits
were forever shattered,
so what seemed to rip and scar me were those
renewed and revealed flashbacks to
the petrified cairns of nightmare and
the spectral visions that clutched and clung
as my newly-integrated soul threw off the scales,
peered through younger eyes,
and felt the clamouring multitudes
resounding through hell on earth
clear to eternity and suffusing
me with shame for the world's
deafening indifference to their fate,
shame for my relative ease,
anger and fear at the jackboots'
resurrected hatred,
wonder at hope and compassion
defiantly blooming
in a wasteland of agony,
humility for sacred acts of faith
in the teeth of profound evil,

and so my presumptuous prayer,
my supplication,
is that this voice channels
even a whisper of the legions
whose courage and suffering
transcends all understanding.

Gossamer
and
Fireflies

The Ant

Halfway down the driveway you were noticed,
some tiny spark catching the eye,
pulling attention to a significant detail
bound together with me in creation's vast web.
Your burden, your prize, proudly
thrust out in front of you: A dead pill bug
seemingly far bigger than you,
but easily borne, at least for stretches.
Pavement cracks; a major obstacle?
Ah, but you flipped around and pulled,
down across up and over, and onward,
transcending apparent limits,
and, in time, into the backyard,
scrambling pulling pushing climbing through
the interminable jungle of the lawn,
bound for a hidden underground realm,
bound for reassimilation by the colony,
bound for insectoid hearth and home.
Heading into my own little realm
I looked up, and wondered.

Nile Sunset

Narrow ribbon of green, besieged by sweeping desert,
spawned by the great river rising
from the depths of the continent,
forever disrupted by the immense Aswan dam,
the ancient course irretrievably changed,
towns drowned, ancient edifices moved,
and yet the waters still striving,
seeking union with the sea far ahead.
Felucca beating against the current, villages hugging the lifeline;
children and water-carriers descend the banks and
watch our amphibious hotel process by,
floating towards the delta, floating through time,
past ancient temples and graves scattered alongside.

The day's fever loosens its grip,
the peace of twilight draws close.
Flint-edged light melts into pastels,
fragrant breeze gently softens and soothes
just two of us absorbed in the magic, the miracle,
the others below decks.
Soon pastels give way to mute fire behind the palms,
flaming bright, then quickly fading to an ember,
surrendering in its turn to night's embrace,
as we will soon surrender to sleep.
Uncountable stars emerge and rise,
standing guard, awaiting sun's return,
and with it, re-awakening.

Foggy Evening

To Jane

Well past dusk, damp but warming,
embracing mist hanging all around,
softening streetlights to luminous pastels,
hushing sounds ahead on Richmond to a loud murmur,
our footsteps gently echoing down the quiet street,
and wombed within the still, laden air
memories of a long ago sojourn over The Pond,
memories of an English winter,
fog floating heavenward from
the Upper Thames and the Cherwell,
rising from my school's rugby pitch,
drifting amongst Oxford's intellectual edifices,
chilling the bones yet warming the heart
with thoughts of hearth and home,
but pulling my mind and soul farther, deeper,
back beyond birth to a distant time,
to the great city on the Lower Thames,
a fetid vapour enveloping the narrow streets,
obscuring night workers and revellers
and cutpurses slinking on their way,
cloaking horses and carts dully rumbling past,
and from every alleyway snake grasping
ghostly claws of excitement and fear,
my companion's laugh urging me back,
back to the pastels and soft echoes,
and the glowing theatre around the corner.

Night Train

Sleep having for an interval stepped away,
I embrace night sounds:
Crickets calling for a mate,
mouse scuttling in the attic,
air wafting from the vents,
when a faint, pulsing hum slips in—
a new visitor has joined the circle.
Warning tones at a crossing a couple of miles off,
another call, louder, and presently in mind's eye and ear
mournful cries become glorious howls><piercing shrieks,
steel wheels hammer out the musical beat
that I at a distance hear now as a driving rumble,
wondering from whence it came and where it's bound.
Soon signals diminish and cease,
bass thrum fades into ambient undertone:
The night train has left my little universe,
but somewhere out in the darkness its journey continues.

Pacific Dream

Searching reciting floating by
hewn and sculpted history standing tall;
gliding searching for translation,
ancient stone remains found
swimming in the ocean, revelation's
low tide awaited.

Startled by the slow drumbeat of
huge pterosaurean wings out of the setting sun,
an out-of-time-and-place quetzalcoatlus
powering north and east, pulling me
through the nascent village
but soaring beyond reach over mountains.

Drawn back to the sea,
tranquil setting now sliced by vehicular
causeway materialized offshore
sporting a quiet-shattering motorcycle;
and out beyond, a cruise ship
slides by, tourists gawk through
road and cars for a glimpse of
remembrance out of reach.

I retreat from the noise
turning yearning for the
magnificent dawn-bound memory.

Gossamer and Fireflies

Deep in nocturnal stillness and quiet when
floating between wakefulness and sleep,
time's illusion falling away, space folding in on itself,
isolation and separation melting in the starlight,
I sense them, like gossamer after a dew
in the gentle light of a calm autumn morning,
or fireflies in a still meadow as dusk slips away
on a warm early summer evening:
Luminous numinous voyages uncounted, uncountable,
all around, near and far, some intersecting and entwining,
some never touching, to each its own trajectory,
origins uncertain, destinations unseen.
All too soon the winds of my restless soulmind
sweep away the fragile portal,
but the ethereal tapestry remains,
perhaps, like gossamer and fireflies,
awaiting a magical moment of rediscovery.

Winter Sunrise

Too early for me in summer,
but now it's there, waiting.
Shadowed blackberry bushes deep in slumber,
squirrels not yet scrounging stray bird seed,
but cardinals will soon touch down and greet
the orange and rose glow stealing in
off to the south, just over the cedar hedge,
behind the wildly growing evergreen on the downslope
and the stately sleeping oak stretching over from
back and left, dangling a few stubborn leaves,
the spreading blush not reaching the patio sundial
but caressing the top of the little arbour
and awakening here and there from
the largesse of yesterday's squall
a delicate opalescence,
bestowing a hushed peace,
a pause between breaths,
the fragile promise of light to come
shimmering on the chilled zephyr
whispering through the pine needles.

Ferry Crossing

Anticipated moment finally, suddenly,
here, open water not my element
but stepping gingerly on board,
a hopeful scan beyond the harbour,
tipsy already with the peaceful
rock and sway at anchor,
exploring our vessel's few
decks and lounges, and startled
by an almighty blast of the horn
as we ease away.

Where should I ride out the crossing?
Perhaps inside; others seem comfortable.
But the air—still and stale,
horizon obscured, floor tilting
this artificial bubble, panic
seeping into all my capillaries.
No.
I must be outside, my own little corner
on the larboard quarter where
the great lake fills my senses,
wind in my face, sealine present, real,
sunlight ricocheting off the dancing depths,
tasting the laden air as I scud along
with cormorants scanning their
realm for unwary sustenance.

I study waves tirelessly chasing
each other and sluicing off the hull,
and notice they have softened slightly,
seagulls now a bit more numerous,
a delicate lightening of the water's hue,
a subtle shift in the prevailing tang,

and look there, gently emerging
through the haze, the waiting shore;
I am nearly home.

Soloist

The leader counts in, tones burst forth
like spring flowers in fast forward,
swirling, linking, dissolving, reforming,
sculpting a cathedral ephemeral,
bass crypt, tenor and alto vaulting,
soaring soprano filigree.
Moment impending, the soloist rises,
flooded by anticipatory tension,
hoping, yet confident,
fusing with the music.
Space created as cathedral
modulates to safety net,
alone, but not, the solo begins,
slowly at first, then building, soaring,
borne up by a nurturing tide
surging through the room,
pulling threads of the ineffable
from spirit's core and weaving
a glorious sonic tapestry
above and beyond, transporting
all to rapturous realms unseen.

Vision complete, the soloist eases down,
melding, reharmonizing. Consummation
achieved, physical sounds cease,
the enchantment echoing still.

Acknowledgements

My sincere thanks to Dr. Karunesh Kumar Agarwal and everyone at Cyberwit, and heartfelt gratitude to Muriel Allingham, Tom Cull, Andreas Gripp, the late Don Hatch, Penn Kemp, Felicia Otchet, Richard-Yves Sitoski, Jane Twynham, Murray Winger and Carole Wray, and my children Sarah Wenn and Andrew Wenn.

My thanks also to the following where versions of the listed poems first appeared:

Beliveau Review: Bluesman, He, Intrusion, Tic, The Ant, Auschwitz Threnody—Pink Triangle, Nocturne, Three Haiku for Warbler Woods; *Big Pond Rumours:* Night Train; *Ekphrastic Review*: On Seeing The Little Shepherdess; *Crossarts' In Between the Lines Exhibit*: Ruminations, Dawn; *LOCP's Fresh Voices*: For a Fellow Traveller; *Journey of the Heart*: Gossamer and Fireflies, Night Flights, Lost Songs, Soloist, Winter Sunrise; *Museum London's 80th Anniversary Exhibit*: Linda; *Open Minds Quarterly*: Down the Rabbit Hole; *Shot Glass Journal*: Mirror; *Synaeresis*: East Wind, David, Sistine Chapel, Foggy Evening, In Memory of Claudius Cossus, Avian Odes—St. Lucian Parrot, Notre-Dame is Burning; *Things That Matter* Anthology: Three Haiku for Algonquin Park, Three Haiku for Turkey Point; *Tuck Magazine*: The Great Wall, Carmanah Walbran, Transgender Anthem; *Watchyourhead*: Avian Odes—Canada Goose; *Wordsfestzine*: Words, Stares, Strawberry Picking, Hatchlings, Storm, Bravery

www.ingramcontent.com/pod-product-compliance
Lightning Source LLC
LaVergne TN
LVHW091453170726
843492LV00001B/170